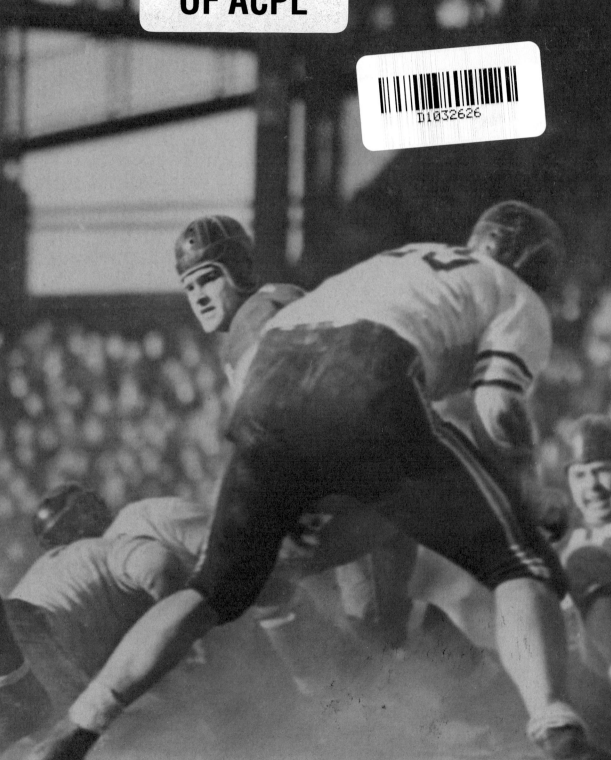

G

PROFESSIONAL FOOTBALL'S GREATEST GAMES

by Paul Michael

PRENTICE-HALL, INC.
ENGLEWOOD CLIFFS, N.J.

Also by Paul Michael
The Academy Awards: A Pictorial History
Humphrey Bogart: The Man and His Films
The American Movies Reference Book: The Sound Era
The Emmy Awards: A Pictorial History

Professional Football's Greatest Games
By Paul Michael
Printed in the United States of America
Prentice-Hall International, Inc., London
Prentice-Hall of Australia, Pty. Ltd., North Sydney
Prentice-Hall of Canada, Ltd., Toronto
Prentice-Hall of India Private Ltd., New Delhi
Prentice-Hall of Japan, Inc., Tokyo

Library of Congress Cataloging in Publication Data
Michael, Paul.
    Professional football's greatest games.
    1. Football stories.   I. Title.
GV954.M5   796.33'2   72-6670
ISBN 0-13-725325-7

ACKNOWLEDGMENTS

1722976

I would like to extend my thanks to the following for their generous help in the preparation of this volume: Dwight Pelkin, without whose help this volume could never have been completed; Donald R. Smith, Pro Football's Hall of Fame; Don Weiss, The National Football League; Dave Boss, National Football League Properties, Inc.; Dan Desmond, Chicago Bears Football Club; Don Smith, The New York Giants; Mr. Barton Silverman; Frank R. Ramos, New York Jets Football Club, Inc.; Charles Martin, Philadelphia *Evening* and *Sunday Bulletin;* Eugene Ferrara, New York *Daily News;* Chuck Lane, Green Bay Packers; Bill Hamilton, Kansas City Chiefs Football Club; Curt Mosher, Dallas Cowboys Football Club; G. J. Christophel, The Redskins of the National Football League; Larry A. Belonger, Green Bay *Press-Gazette;* Clement G. Vitek, Baltimore *Sun;* John Rammel, Milwaukee *Journal;* Suzanne Caster, San Francisco *Chronicle;* John F. McLeod, Washington *Daily News;* Frances Barger, Dallas *Morning News;* Shirley Baig, *The New York Times;* Earl Pruce, Baltimore *News* and *American;* Nathan Wallack, Cleveland Browns; George Bartholomew, Houston *Chronicle;* Ken Ford, New Castle, Indiana *Courier-Times;* Harold F. Fuller, Jr., Suburban Journals, Inc.; Bob Hammel, Bloomington *Herald-Telephone;* Ron Reid, San Mateo *Times;* Phil Angelo, *Darien Review;* Harry Fisher, Huntington *Herald-Dispatch;* Jack R. Stein, Denison *Herald;* Ed Plaisted, *Sun-Tattler;* Jim Laughter, Smithfield *Herald;* Miles E. Rank Jr., Barnesboro *Star;* Terry E. Bache, Sam Fausto, *Evening Chronicle,* Uhrichsville, Ohio; James Bradbury, Cottage Grove *Sentinel;* Walter G. Anderson, Baldwyn *News;* Casey Kozminski, Houma *Courier;* Bob Willmer, Terrebonne *Press;* Kim Mohan, Beloit *Daily News;* Alice Carnahan, Eudora *Enterprise;* A. Scott Clark, Mexico *Evening Ledger;* Bob Sparberg, Peru, Indiana *Daily Tribune;* Bill Van Horne, Wheeling *News-Register;* Roy Riley, Opelika-Auburn *Daily News;* Paul L. Golias, Times-Leader *Evening News;* Ned Frear, Bedford

Gazette; Ted R. Olsen, Goldendale *Sentinel;* Henry Dolecki, Derrick Publishing Company; John W. Bozadjian, Willimantic *Daily Chronicle;* Charles J. Tiano, *The Daily Freeman;* Dean Eagle, Louisville *Courier-Journal;* Tom Huntington, Berwick Enterprise; James Alan Coogan, *Turkey Mountain Gobbler;* Harley Bowers, Macon *Telegraph;* Tommy Hallum, Calhoun County *Journal;* Gene Cuneo, Erie *Times;* Mike Brown, Huntington *Herald-Dispatch;* Robert J. Weirich, Marion *Star;* James V. Debevec, Cleveland *American-Home;* Dennis Hernet, Manitowoc *Herald-Times;* Bob Maisel, *Baltimore Sun;* Bill Richardson, *Kansas City Star;* Joe Marcin, *The Sporting News;* and the other sports editors and writers who took part in the poll that selected the games included in the book.

INTRODUCTION

This book started with an argument—and, I suppose, it will lead to many controversies from one end of the country to the other. It started innocently enough.

Quite without thinking about the consequences of my actions, I happened to say to a friend: "I think the Giants-Colts 'sudden-death' overtime game of 1958 was the greatest pro football game ever played." The argument that took place was never settled—but I did manage to lose my friend!

That started me thinking. What games did people consider great—and why? I quickly discovered that there was no such thing as a quiet discussion of the subject. Everyone I spoke with had a different opinion—and at least two dozen reasons for his opinion.

There is a Pro Football Hall of Fame to enshrine great players and great coaches—but, as far as I know, there has never, until now, been an attempt to chronicle professional football's greatest games. Perhaps no one had the courage.

But who could make the choices? The answer seemed obvious to me: the newspaper and magazine sports editors and writers of the country—men who know the sport—men who are hopefully more objective than fans like you or me. And so to work.

An impartial survey of 2,340 newspaper and magazine sports editors and writers was conducted by mail to select Professional Football's Greatest Games.

Official Ballots were mailed to every daily newspaper in the nation and to all magazines that regularly cover football.

Each editor and writer was asked simply to list those games he considered "great"; the basis of the selections was left up to the individual. He was not required to select games in the order of their "greatness"—he was not limited to selecting a specific number of games.

In all, 1,437 Official Ballots were returned. Some listed only one game, others had up to seventeen different games listed.

In order to simplify the scoring, a single point was awarded to a game each time it was named on an individual Official Ballot. Here are the games selected, and the number of points garnered:

Points	Game		
1,032	Green Bay Packers	vs Dallas Cowboys	December 31, 1967
930	Baltimore Colts	vs New York Giants	December 28, 1958
800	Chicago Bears	vs Washington Redskins	December 8, 1940
762	Cleveland Browns	vs Philadelphia Eagles	September 16, 1950
700	Chicago Bears	vs New York Giants	December 9, 1934
684	New York Jets	vs Baltimore Colts	January 12, 1969
600	Cleveland Browns	vs Los Angeles Rams	December 24, 1950
530	Chicago Cardinals	vs Chicago Bears	November 28, 1929
517	New York Giants	vs Chicago Bears	December 17, 1933
496	Washington Redskins	vs Chicago Bears	December 12, 1937
428	Cleveland Rams	vs Washington Redskins	December 16, 1945
411	Detroit Lions	vs Cleveland Browns	December 27, 1953
164	Philadelphia Eagles	vs Green Bay Packers	December 26, 1960
152	New York Giants	vs Notre Dame All Stars	December 14, 1930
80	Dallas Texans	vs Houston Oilers	December 23, 1962
36	Dallas Cowboys	vs Green Bay Packers	January 1, 1967
18	Green Bay Packers	vs Baltimore Colts	December 26, 1965
14	Green Bay Packers	vs New York Giants	December 11, 1938
2	Chicago Bears	vs San Francisco 49ers	December 12, 1965
2	Green Bay Packers	vs Chicago Bears	September 15, 1935
2	Green Bay Packers	vs Beloit Fairies	November 23, 1919
2	Kansas City Chiefs	vs Oakland Raiders	January 4, 1970
2	New York Giants	vs Chicago Bears	December 6, 1925

Every game that was listed on at least two Official Ballots—23 games—has been included in this volume. In addition, 38 other games were listed on at least one Official Ballot.

There were two interesting sidelights to the survey.

First, 19 different teams are represented, as well as one college team, the Notre Dame All Stars of 1930. The teams and the number of games in which they appear are listed here:

Chicago Bears	8	Chicago Cardinals	1
Green Bay Packers	7	Cleveland Rams	1
New York Giants	6	Detroit Lions	1
Baltimore Colts	3	Notre Dame All Stars	1
Washington Redskins	3	Dallas Texans	1
Cleveland Browns	3	Houston Oilers	1
Dallas Cowboys	2	San Francisco 49ers	1
Philadelphia Eagles	2	Beloit Fairies	1
New York Jets	1	Oakland Raiders	1
Los Angeles Rams	1	Kansas City Chiefs	1

The other interesting sidelight is the fact that games from every decade since the beginning of professional football have been selected—a span of 51 years—from November 23, 1919 when the Green Bay Packers played the Beloit Fairies—to January 4, 1970 when Oakland played Kansas City.

One word about the style of the book. Most of us read about professional football games in our daily newspapers—without much historical perspective. We are interested in who won, who scored the points, the most exciting plays, the mishaps, the sidelights, the drama of the games. There is something especially exciting about picking up the morning paper and reading the story—something exciting about its immediacy.

Hopefully, this book has been written from the same point of view. As you read about each of the games in this book— *Professional Football's Greatest Games*—I hope that you get the feeling of excitement you would have gotten if you had actually read the game story—the very day after it was played.

Paul Michael
New York, N.Y.

CONTENTS

(In order of their selection)

GREEN BAY PACKERS VS. DALLAS COWBOYS
(Game played December 31, 1967)

GREEN BAY, WIS. (Jan. 1, 1968)—What do you do when it's 13 degrees below zero, you have the ball on icy footing on the 1-yard line, you're behind 17-14, and there are only 16 seconds left to play? That was the decision confronting the Green Bay Packers here yesterday in icebound Lambeau Field against the Dallas Cowboys in the National Football League championship game. The Super Bowl awaits the winner, but it cannot possibly top the Ice Bowl that was played here.

What the Packers did in that abominable 13 below zero, on ice, from a yard out, and trailing with no time remaining to score if they failed—was to score, and the quarterback Bart Starr doing it himself. Behind two crunching blocks on frozen turf and on a play that everyone knew would be the Packers' last try, Starr dug in for just enough traction to hurl himself into the end zone and give his team the points needed for a 21-17 victory and the championship.

Just 13 seconds remained when he lunged in.

For the 50,861 numbed spectators huddling in misery, the end came with a mingling of hysteria and sheer relief. They had sat for 2 and a half hours swathed in sleeping bags, ski masks, and multilayers of clothing—and in the gray-shrouded late minutes of the game had had a foreboding of doom for their Packers.

Dallas had seized the lead seconds after the final quarter began and had clung to it until yielding the ball to Green Bay with less than 5 minutes to go and the goal line 68 yards distant. And with the bitter, penetrating cold an invisible ally as well as time. But the Packers, down 17-14, rallied themselves for one last charge and drove those 68 yards to score and win. When Starr "snuck in" on a wedge play behind the defense-shoving, skidding blocks of guard Jerry Kramer and center Ken Bowman, he gave Green Bay an unprecedented third consecutive NFL crown—and another shot at the Super Bowl, this time against the Oakland Raiders. A year ago, it had whipped Kansas City, another upstart of the old American Football League, 35-10 in the first Super Bowl.

1

Crucial though every play was on that relentless closing march, it was the last few that made for so dramatic a climax. Nine plays after they began their drive, the Packers were on the Dallas 3—with only 54 seconds to play. They only needed 2 yards for a vital first down. Time had been called to save whatever seconds could be saved. Then the officials waved play on again:

54 seconds left: Starr called on Donny Anderson. Anderson plunged in on a simple dive play, got the 2 yards—and the first down. The ball now rested on the 1-yard line. The Packers lined up hurriedly. Dallas grimly dug in.

30 seconds left: Again Starr called on Anderson to get it, but this time Donny slid on the icy turf, barely getting back to the line of scrimmage to avoid a disastrous loss. No gain, a play wasted—and before Starr could call time, precious moments had elapsed. Bart now was very much aware of the precarious footing.

20 seconds left: Once more, it was Anderson. This time Starr called for a dive play with power—but again Anderson slipped and this time almost fumbled. Starr recalled later in the dressing room, "As I started to hand off, he slipped forward on the ball—and he just barely got back to the line." So once more—now for the last chance with no more time-outs left—Starr quickly stopped the clock.

16 seconds left: Now it was decision time on the Packer bench. There were still 2 downs left, there was still only 1 yard to go, but there probably was time enough for only 1 play. With players piling up on every play—and Dallas, extremely aware of the time situation, undoubtedly being very slow in unpiling—the chances of running off the fourth-down play were at best dubious. (As somebody said, "They would have just sat on Starr for a while" on the next play—and with no time-outs left, that could have been it.)

So Starr conferred with Coach Vince Lombardi on the sidelines.

There was no serious consideration of a field goal on the next play—even though it might have been the final one. The determination was to "go for it." The field-goal unit was ready on the sidelines, however, set to dash in should Lombardi so order. But as Vince admitted after the game, "I don't know if we would have had time for another play; it was just a gamble we took." He also said that he did not want to go for the field goal and a tie. "I didn't figure the people in the stands wanted to sit around in the cold any longer; I do have some compassion, though I've been accused of having none." With only 16 seconds and no time-outs remaining, there was also, of course, the question of whether or not the kicking unit could have dashed the 40 to 50 angling yards, positioned themselves, and then gotten off the kick. Starr admitted uncertainty about it—and also revealed that he "hadn't even given a field goal a thought." Press-box consensus held that there would *not* have been time to get off such a fourth-down kick had the next play failed.

The only decision, then, was which play to call—which running play. Anderson again was the first thought, but then a successful fullback wedge play by Chuck Mercein earlier in the game was recalled. And so a wedge it would be—No. 31. Kramer was sure he would somehow get the footing necessary for a block.

There is a contradiction at this point, however, as to what really happened.

Kramer in the dressing room recalled Starr as saying that "we were going to run a thirty-one wedge with the same blocking as always except that he wouldn't hand off to either the halfback or the fullback. He said 'and we darn well better make it.' " The articulate lineman added, "He was going to go for the hole just inside me, just off my left shoulder. Kenny Bowman and I were supposed to move big Jethro Pugh out of the way. The ground was giving me trouble, the footing was bad down near the goal line, but I dug my cleats in, got a firm hold with my right foot, and we got down in position, and Bart called the 'hut' signal. Jethro was on my inside shoulder, my left shoulder. I slammed into Jethro hard, coming off the ball as fast as I ever have in my life; all he had time to do was raise his left arm—he didn't even get it up all the way and I charged into him. His body was a little high, the way we'd noticed in the movies, and with Bowman's help I moved him outside. Willie Townes, next to Jethro, was down low—very low. He was supposed to come in low and close toward the middle; he was low, but he didn't close. He might have filled the hole, but he didn't—and Bart churned into the opening and stretched and fell and landed over the goal line."

Starr himself had a somewhat different recollection of his

3

decision to keep the ball rather than hand off to Mercein—or, for that matter, Anderson: "As I was calling the play, the thought flashed through my mind that regardless of how good the block is, if Mercein should slip, he wouldn't be able to get to the hole in time. I also thought of the time we scored on the same kind of icy field against the 49ers in Milwaukee a year earlier with a sneak. So I called the wedge play, but I didn't tell anybody that I wasn't going to give the ball to Mercein. I felt I could just hug the block in there. Because of an upright stance, I felt I would have better footing—just one step and go in right on top. And I sneaked it in there. I guess the good Lord takes care of you in things like that. The thought just flashed through my mind."

It took just 3 seconds for Bowman to snap the ball back to Starr and for the lunge into the end zone. The clock stopped automatically. Had the play not gone for a touchdown, time would have kept running, and it is doubtful whether Green Bay could have arranged itself for one last play and run it off before the gun cracked.

The kickoff soared into the end zone, leaving Dallas just 13 seconds. Two hurried passes fell incomplete to end it.

Dramatic as that final minute was at the 3-yard line and inside, the game itself had been a tremendous one all the way—especially in the last 5 minutes when Green Bay was faced with the desperate situation of having to take it all the way or lose.

That it was an inspired drive is evident: It began on the Green Bay 32 with 4:54 showing on the scoreboard clock towering over the darkening stadium. Willie Wood had just run back a punt 9 yards. Said Kramer of the Packer thinking at this point, "Maybe this is the year we don't make it, that it all ends—but I know every guy made up his mind that if we were going down, we were going down trying." And of the drive that was about to begin, Mercein—picked up by the Packers from the Washington Redskins' taxi squad after the eighth game of the season—was to say later in the dressing room, "I'll never forget that last drive. To see it must have been great, but to be in it and to feel it was just something else. I don't know how to explain it."

The march got under way with a pass, a play-action pass designed to hold the rush, crossing pattern with the hopes of

4

freeing a receiver. It didn't work that way, but it did free Anderson on the outside beyond the range of the linebacker. It went for 6. Then Mercein slanted off tackle, and the Packers had their first down on the 45. Next Starr hit Boyd Dowler on the weak side for another first down on the Dallas 42. Dowler was shaken up on the play and was replaced by veteran Max McGee.

Then came a crushing play, a big 9-yard loss by Anderson, as huge (6-4 and 265 pounds) Willie Townes burst through to nail him back on the Packer 49. It fired up the Cowboys and depressed the crowd—but not the Packers. Starr later commented on the situation in the dressing room: "We're not going to throw on every down; we don't have all the time in the world, but we don't have to panic. But a big loss like that is the thing you try to guard against. Now you've got to throw it. It really put us in a bind."

So Starr threw. Again to young running back Anderson. He latched onto the ball in the right flat, eluded linebacker Chuck Howley with the help of the slippery footing, and got a dozen yards. And once more Starr went to Anderson in the air, this time for 9 and a first down.

But now the clock was at 1:35. And the ball on the 30. Starr disclosed his thinking again. "We're in a formation where Mercein's responsibility is to help move the defense so you can free the other receivers. Mercein was not covered very closely and was allowed to get outside and beyond the linebacker. So he's an open receiver—he's got to be the logical choice. The play maybe should have gained seven, eight, or ten yards—but we pick up nineteen and it puts us in great position because Mercein was able to get out of bounds with the thing at the Dallas eleven to stop the clock." The pass was off to the left flat, and although Mercein later said he thought he had a chance to go all the way, he just "ran out of field." But his running out-of-bounds ultimately proved to be vital.

So now the clock showed just 1:11 to play, and the ball was on the 11. Again Starr outlined the situation: "The next one is a very critical play, because it puts us in position to score. It's a lot tougher to score from the eleven, of course, than it is from the three. The reason we called this particular play, which saw Mercein sweep our left side for eight yards, was because earlier in the game

Chuck told us he couldn't make a block on Bob Lilly because he pursued on such a flat plane. If Lilly's chasing the guard, we reasoned, he can't defend against the play too. He did just what we expected, so Mercein went through the area that Lilly left—we didn't even block Lilly on the play. The big responsibility on this one is Bob Skoronski's block. He must make a great block on the defensive end, which he did."

That's the way Starr calculated things—and the way it was executed. Mercein slammed through on the quick opener all the way to the 3 and from there, in those final 54 seconds, it was Anderson-Anderson-Anderson-Starr. "I think if I'd had a little better footing, I might have been able to drive the last couple of yards," Mercein opined. "It was a great call by Bart. It was a 'give' play, and it looks just like a play on which the fullback blocks and the give is to the halfback going wide. Lilly committed himself right away and chased the guard . . . you either run right behind the guy or he gets you because nobody blocks him."

But the game obviously was not all played in the last 5 minutes. There were 55 other minutes of importance on this day of savage weather on which the wind factor made the true temperature closer to 27 below zero than the registered 13 degrees.

When the Cowboys won the toss, one press-box wag quipped that "Dallas won the toss and elected to go home." What Dallas did do was elect to receive.

What Green Bay did was score the first time it got the ball, taking over on its 18 after forcing a Cowboy punt. It moved 82 yards in 16 plays (including 2 Dallas penalties), with Carroll Dale making 2 good catches for gains of 17 and 15 to spearhead the march. His second catch put the ball on the 9-yard line, Anderson banged the middle for 1, and then Starr flipped to Dowler up the middle for the TD. Don Chandler's placement then made it 7-0 with 8:50 elapsed in the ball game.

Early in the second quarter, the Packers swept 65 yards on a 4-play quickie assault. Three rushes put the ball on the Dallas 43, and with third and 1 Starr fooled the Cowboys by pitching to Dowler. The lanky 6-5 end stretched hard to get a seemingly overthrown ball, pulled it in on the run, and outran Mel Renfro for the score: 14-0 and only 2:41 gone in the period.

When Green Bay's Herb Adderley intercepted a short pass by Don Meredith and ran it back 15 yards, the Packers were on the Dallas 32 barely a minute later! A TD here, and the game could have been blown wide open. Even a field goal could have made catching the Packers very, very difficult.

But the Packers got neither.

After 2 plays failed, Starr was dumped back on the 42 by George Andrie, and it was a punting, not a threatening, situation. Dallas at this point was in command defensively, its vigorous Doomsday Defense actually throwing the Packers for a total of 29 yards in losses on their last 12 plays of the half. They continued to put extreme pressure on Starr as part of Coach Tom Landry's game plan (the Cowboys got to Starr 8 times in all, nailing him for 76 yards), and finally with just 4 minutes left in the half, made one of their pass rushes pay off. With the ball on the 26, big Townes crashed into Starr and jarred the ball loose; Andrie simply scooped it up and pranced half a dozen yards into the end zone for a touchdown. When Danny Villanueva booted the PAT, the gap was closed to 14-7 and the game no longer was a Packer romp.

But the half wasn't over yet.

When Willie Wood fumbled a punt return with 1:50 remaining, Phil Clark pounced on the ball on the Green Bay 17. While the Cowboys couldn't move the ball deeper than the 13, they nevertheless wound up with points as Villanueva kicked a 21-yard field goal with 36 seconds to go, making it a tight 14-10.

Twice Dallas threatened in the third quarter, but twice failed to score. Don Meredith moved his team nicely from its 11 all the way to the Packer 18, but Green Bay stiffened; when Meredith had to run with the ball in the face of a strong pass rush, he was hit by Lee Roy Caffey, and Adderley stopped him on the 22 to avert that threat. On their next series, the Cowboys moved from Green Bay's 46 to its 30 before Caffey racked Meredith for a 9-yard loss and forced a field-goal try by Villanueva from the 47 that fell short. Two minutes later the period ended.

Eight seconds after the fourth period began, Dallas had scored and was out front for the first time in the ball game. They were on the 50, having fair-caught a punt on their own 45 and then shot fullback Don Perkins into the line for 5 on first down as the third

7

quarter ended. With this ripe second-and-5 situation, Meredith cagily called for a halfback option play, with versatile Dan Reeves getting the ball. Reeves swung out, then arched a long spiral upfield—and speedy Lance Rentzel raced under it, pulled it in on the 20, and beat safety Tom Brown to the end zone (although Bob Jeter admitted to "goofing" in not dropping back on the play). Rentzel said later: "That's a great play; Danny Reeves makes it go—he throws the pass real well. We've had three touchdowns and a couple of forty yard gains on it, and we've only used it about ten times. I watched for Wood to press in and take himself out of the play; then it was just between me and Bob Jeter." Villanueva kicked the extra point and it was a 17-14 ball game.

Six minutes went by before the Packers had any real chance to score—and they failed when Chandler's field-goal try from the 40 dropped short. Then Dallas took over, moved the ball for a couple of first downs as Meredith used up nearly 5 more minutes, and finally had to punt from its own 38.

He thus gave the Packers that one last chance. A chance they didn't pass up.

As a beaming Vince Lombardi said in the dressing room, "This is what the Packers are all about—what we did in the last two minutes. They don't do it for individual glory, they do it because they respect each other and have a feeling for the other fellow."

Or as Donny Anderson put it: "Beautiful, man, just beautiful . . . "

The Scoring:

Dallas	0	10	0	7	—	17
Green Bay	7	7	0	7	—	21

GB—Dowler 8, Starr pass (Chandler kick)
GB—Dowler 46, Starr pass (Chandler kick)
Dal.—Andrie 7, return of Starr funble (Villanueva kick)
Dal.—FG Villanueva 21
Dal.—Rentzel 50, Reeves pass (Villanueva kick)
GB—Starr 1, run (Chandler kick)

GREEN BAY PACKERS VS. DALLAS COWBOYS, 1967

The Statistics:

	GB	Dal.
First downs	18	11
Rushing yardage	80	92
Passing yardage	115	100
Passes	14-24	11-26
Own passes intercepted	0	1
Punting	8-29	8-39.1
Fumbles lost	2	1
Penalties	2-10	7-58
Offensive plays (including times thrown)	64	60

Individual Statistics:

Rushing

Green Bay—Anderson 18 attempts for 35 yards, Mercein 6 for 20, Williams 4 for 13, Wilson 3 for 11, Starr 1 for 1.

Dallas—Perkins 17 attempts for 51 yards, Reeves 13 for 42, Meredith 1 for 9, Clarke 1 for minus 8, Baynham 1 for minus 2.

Passing

Green Bay—Starr 24 attempts for 14 completions and 191 yards.

Dallas—Meredith 25 attempts for 10 completions and 59 yards (1 intercepted), Reeves 1 for 1 and 50 yards.

Receiving

Green Bay—Dowler 4 completions for 77 yards, Anderson 4 for 44, Dale 3 for 44, Mercein 2 for 22, Williams 1 for 4.

Dallas—Hayes 3 completions for 16 yards, Reeves 3 for 11, Clarke 2 for 24, Rentzel 2 for 61, Baynham 1 for 3.

II

BALTIMORE COLTS VS. NEW YORK GIANTS
(Game played December 28, 1958)

NEW YORK, N. Y. (Dec. 29, 1958)—This was one of the great ones.

Sometime, somewhere—perhaps!—a greater game of football will be played, but don't say that to the 64,175 enraptured fans at Yankee Stadium yesterday. Nor to the millions who watched on television.

For Sunday's tremendous 23-17 Baltimore Colts victory over the New York Giants will surely go down in professional—perhaps all—football history as one of the classics if not the ultimate game. It won for the Colts the National Football League (that is, "world") championship; but that in itself isn't the big thing, for such titles have been won many times before—and, indeed, by closer margins. What stamps Sunday's game as The Great One is that for the first time ever, a championship football game was won in "sudden death." Overtime. Extra innings. For 4 full quarters the two NFL divisional champions had fought to a 17-all deadlock (tied on a 20-yard Colt field goal with just 7 seconds of those first 60 minutes remaining) and then continued their dramatic battling for another 8 and a quarter minutes of ultra-tension before Baltimore finally ended it.

The greatest game? Not just an average fan, but no less a grid notable than NFL Commissioner Bert Bell, characterized the game as "the greatest I've ever seen"—and enthralled spectators could be heard muttering the same thing as they left the park long after it was over. Even the crestfallen New Yorkers.

So it was a great one. And not just because of the unprecedented sudden death.

Besides being two fine football teams, best of their divisions, and both playing cracking hard and good football, they put on a stupendous show all the way. Baltimore quickly took charge, generally dominated the early going, and held a solid 14-3 half-time lead. Then the defense-oriented New Yorkers clawed back, made a magnificent game-saving goal-line stand, and scored twice to go astonishingly into the last 7 seconds of the game leading by 3 points. Whereupon Steve Myhra kicked his oh-so-crucial field goal, and it was overtime. It finally ended with dynamic Alan "The Horse" Ameche ripping through a huge hole for the final yard after the incomparable Johnny Unitas had directed the Colts 80 yards on an irresistible, brilliantly conceived and executed march the first time Baltimore got the ball.

Making for constant tension and something unique in football was the knowledge that any broken play that turned the ball over to the other team in the unusual sudden-death situation could drastically change the whole "ball of wax"—and so every play was exquisitely vital in those 8 minutes and 15 seconds of overtime. New York had the first opportunity in the sudden-death period but after receiving the kickoff ran 3 frustrated plays (one a near miss that could have ended it) and punted. Baltimore got the ball deep on its 20, and 13 plays later was home.

That culminating TD drive was obviously the money-winner (a record $4,718.77 for the champions compared with $3,111.33 for the losers), but for pure drama it was the Colts' final surge before the end of the regulation time that was most gripping. This was a fantastic assault ("march" is hardly the word) as they swept 86 yards in less than 2 minutes in a George S. Patton blitzkrieg movement. It was relentless and it was fast. It had to be relentless and it had to be fast. So while behind clouting blocks it was Ameche lunging in for the final yard and the victory in overtime, that score-or-else last-quarter drive by the Colts was even more critical and more tingling than the climactic payoff. It "had to be or else," whereas the sudden-death threat could have been thwarted and the two teams at least would have gone at it for an unlimited period of time. With 1:56 left in the game, 86 yards to go, and down by 3 points, the Colts had to score—*had* to score!—in regulation "or else."

The situation:

> Time Left—1:56
> Yards to go—86
> Points Needed—3 to tie, more to win.

What did the Colts do? They tied. Then went on to win. Overtime was the frosting, but the cake was something special in itself—mightily special.

As the end of the regular game neared, Baltimore had gotten to the Giant 27 and was obviously threatening—but here some vigorous defensive plays by such as Andy Robustelli and Jim Katcavage tossed Unitas back for huge losses. Baltimore reluctantly had to punt—and pray (and battle).

It was here that New York almost put it away, but Baltimore came up with the big play just when it had to get it. With third and 4 on the New York 40, Frank Gifford broke to the right and burst ahead. A fired-up Baltimore defense crushed him down within inches of the needed first down that could have decided it. It was a huge, pulsing pile-up, at the bottom of which was big 6-foot-4 and 245-pound Gino Marchetti of the Colts. When the officials finally ruled the ball dead it was less than a foot short of the first down, and the Giants had to punt. They had to take Marchetti off on a stretcher—but his valiant defensing had probably made the difference in the ball game, although he wouldn't play again that day, for his Colts had taken over—his "offensive Colts." New York had to punt, and Don Chandler booted it well, Carl Taseff signaled for a fair catch on his 14.

Eighty-six yards and less than 2 minutes from either a score or the end of the game.

Four seconds were lost on the first play when Unitas missed on an opening pass. He lost another 22 seconds on the next play—but this time gained 11 yards (and a precious first down) on a strike to Lenny Moore. Then another pass missed—and more seconds ticked away. He threw one to Ray Berry and the limp-footed, great-feinting end snatched it for 25 big yards. Another clutch play. Twice more he and Berry got together on passes for 16 and then 21 yards. To the consternation of New York fans and the delirium of Baltimore boosters the ball was now on the New York 13. But only 7 seconds were left.

It had been a majestic drive. A Unitas drive. Here was a young man of 25, repeatedly rebuffed at getting a chance to prove his prowess to college and pro teams—finally snatched up by the Colts from the "sandlots" of semipro football and now quarterbacking a team playing for the championship of the world. He was utterly unruffled, supremely cocky and cool, a knowing master in his trade of running a ball team, of mixing passes and runs to gain yards and score points.

Unitas knew that the Giants were obviously concerned about a "bomb" that would gain immediate gobs of yardage—and so he adroitly concentrated on Berry for relatively short (but sure) gains. Berry in his perfectionist way caught the ball and each time ran with it for more yards than the pass itself—once on a flashy flying catch—to set up his team for "position." His 3 catches on the ultimate drive and Unitas' daring strike throws were all musts.

Moreover, Unitas, like all great passers, altered his traditional pass-routes that were successful during the season. With two prime receivers in Berry and L. G. Dupre, he switched things to befuddle the Giant defenders repeatedly—and this was probably the finest defending corps in the league. He called his plays and he hit his targets magnificently. And his targets did their job too: On the critical catch that set up the field goal, Berry ran straight for ace defender Karl Karilivacz and when co-defender Harland Svare swung over to the equally dangerous Dupre, his hook-in and subsequent spin-away got him loose for 21 biggies to the 13.

With so little time left (7 seconds) the Colts didn't bother huddling but went straightaway into field-goal formation. The angle wasn't the greatest, but Myhra was confident that he could boot it true. He said in the locker room after the game that he was "really only worried about a good snap from center so I could get a fair chance at the goal." While the attention naturally focused on Myhra as the kicker, two other Colts in particular had critical roles in the play—center Buzz Nutter and holder George Shaw. Nutter ordinarily would not have been called on to make the snap, but regular center Lee Sanford was injured on the second play of the game and was not out there. Shaw couldn't help but nervously recall that an earlier field-goal attempt had been blocked by the Giants—a grim knowledge that must have affected not only him, but Myhra and the whole Baltimore squad as well. But Nutter snapped it crisply, Shaw positioned the ball precisely, and Myhra stepped into it as the Colts' line thrust back the charging Giants.

14

Myhra later admitted to "looking up" to see where the kick went, but he needn't have; it sailed through the uprights and the game was tied.

With Colt captain Marchetti on the sidelines with a fractured ankle suffered in that crucial defensive play several minutes earlier, Unitas went out with Giant co-captains Kyle Rote and Bill Svoboda for the all-important coin flip. He called it wrong, New York won the toss, and chose to receive the kickoff.

The Giants thus obtained the first advantage, but were unable to capitalize on it. Frank Gifford got 4 yards on the first play, and then Charley Conerly neatly faked a draw play that enabled end Bob Schnelker to get clear only to have the pass miss its target. Schnelker desperately dove for the ball but couldn't quite nab it. Again Conerly wanted to go to the air, but with his receivers covered, the 37-year old quarterback had to run it himself. He almost made it. But first linebacker Bill Pellington hit him, then middle guard Don Schinnick busted him from the side, stopping him barely a foot shy of the first down. The Giants now decided to punt. Baltimore took over on its 20—a long way from scoring territory but at least it had the football, and this time there was no worry about the clock running out.

Unitas took the Colts those 80 yards in 13 plays. Peerless passer though he was, Unitas nevertheless wanted to stay on the ground as much as possible to reduce the chances of an interception. On the very first play he shot Dupre sweeping to the right for an even 10 yards and a first down. Next he went to the pass, this time sending Lenny Moore far upfield on a game-breaker, but Lindon Crow was just able to tip the ball enough that the sprinting Moore couldn't latch onto it. Then a draw to Dupre almost broke him clear. On the next play Ameche got free briefly in the left flat and took Unitas' swing pass for a first down at the 40.

Now Unitas went back to the same play that began the series with Dupre this time cutting inside for 3 yards. But the next play was nearly disastrous. Big tackle Dick Modzelewski slipped his block, stormed in, and dropped Unitas for an 8-yard loss. (Said the Colt QB, "I had a pass play called but Moe just wrapped me up.") That made it third and 15 and if the Colts were to keep their drive alive they had to come up with a big play here.

15

They did. They went into a formation set up specifically for the playoff game but which had yet to be used—a slot right with Moore in the slot. But he couldn't elude his man, and Unitas had to look for secondary receiver, Ray Berry. Checking out the other side of the field, he found that not only had his blockers kept the Giants out beautifully but Karilivacz had slipped while covering Berry. Unitas waved Berry on for deeper yardage. He button-hooked, and in a few strides had 20 big yards and a first down in New York territory. That was one of the big plays of the drive.

Then came another one. Modzelewski's charging tactics worked against him this time. As Unitas said later, "he was blowing in too fast to suit me and I figured they were right for a trap." He called a play that had been run earlier in the game designed for short yardage. Modzelewski slammed through again but guard Art Spinney sliced across behind center and took him out with a crushing trap block. Unitas handed off to Ameche who fired through the huge gap left by "Moe's" rush, and when George Preas cut down Sam Huff the burly fullback had running room. The play went for 23 yards, all the way down to the 20. (Unitas later elaborated on the call in the locker room. "Those Giant linemen were 'blowing in' on me pretty good and when we noticed that Huff was laying back just a bit for pass protection we figured that Modzelewski would come flying through there. He did and everything worked out the way it was supposed to—Ameche went clean up the middle.")

No gain by Dupre on a try off right tackle was followed by a routine slant pass to Berry. Now the ball was inside the 10, and the Giants were obviously in grave trouble. Next Unitas shot Ameche into the line on a slant off right tackle; but when he altered direction and instead dove up the middle, Huff cut him down. It gained a bare yard.

Unitas could well have been second-guessed on the following play, for with the ball well in punch-it-in range he decided to fool the Giants with an audacious pass to end Jim Mutscheller in the right flat. The cagey Colt quarterback reasoned that New York would surely be playing to defend against a run, so he ordered Mutscheller to cut quickly for the corner. He got past his man, Unitas flipped it to him, and Baltimore was on the one. Had the ball been poorly thrown or had defender Cliff Livingston

16

anticipated the unorthodox call, the Giants might well have come up with an interception that could have gone all the way. But Unitas did not throw poorly nor did the New Yorkers guess that Baltimore would do anything other than smash for the goal.

Baltimore went over the goal line on the next play. It was all over. No need even for an extra point attempt.

The Giants had gone into a standard goal-line defense, but no matter what their deployment it probably would not have mattered: The call was a power play to Ameche, and it is doubtful that anybody could have stopped the rampaging of "The Horse" with that scant yard to go. Mutscheller and Moore made two thunderous blocks on incoming secondary men ahead of the play, Alex Sandusky and Preas blasted the hole at the scrimmage line, and Ameche shot through. ("They couldn't have stopped him if we'd needed ten yards," Unitas said afterwards.) Actually, the play was something of a fooler at that, inasmuch as Baltimore's usual preference had been to shoot over left tackle Jim Parker. This time the point was right tackle—and the hole was bulldozer wide.

Ameche literally never touched ground after bursting into the end zone as the delirious Baltimore fans (who in anticipation of the TD had been crowding ever closer to the field— scooped him up and carried him around the gridiron while pandemonium broke loose. Long after the exhausted but jubilant players had wrested themselves loose and gained the sanctuary of the clubhouse the Baltimore "fan-atics" were still surging back and forth over Yankee Stadium. Goalposts simply didn't exist after the game.

But the first 50-odd minutes—for there *was* a game before sudden death and those dramatic last two minutes of regulation— made a dandy game. Only 3 points were scored in the first quarter, those by New York on a 36-yard field goal by Pat Summerall late in the going. But twice on the drive the Giants might well have picked up 6—or 7. Back Alex Webster was in the clear and down deep in Colt territory but a well-thrown Conerly pass failed to connect when he slipped, the ball sailing harmlessly overhead. And Gifford broke away for a big 38-yard run that set up the field-goal attempt; he might have gone all the way had he not been nudged off-stride on a desperation tackle losing an irretrievable step. Either play could have "gone," neither did—and so New York wound up with a field goal.

Baltimore also tried a 3-pointer that quarter, but linebacker Huff got a clear shot and blocked it—something the Colts were to rectify later in their game-tying kick.

The second quarter was all Baltimore's, abetted by Giant fumbles—both by Gifford. With Unitas devastating the New York defenses on shrewd plays and great passing (behind marvelous blocking protection by the likes of Parker, Preas, Sandusky, and Spinney in the line and his fine backfield protectors), the Colts scored twice for a lopsided half-time bulge. Ameche banged over from the 2 for the first score and Unitas faked out the Giants for the next as he sent his Horse into the line but pitched to Berry instead for a 15-yard payoff. This was set up by a seemingly similar play on which the Giants' defensive back Jim Patton stopped Ameche but then was "frozen" when the next play kept the same play but switched to the air. Myhra's PATs ran it to 14-3 at the half.

Baltimore quickly threatened to put it away as the second half began. Unitas hit his recievers with precision to guide the Colts on an early drive that seemed to produce a certain score—and 21-3 would surely be a certain victory. But with first down on the 3, Baltimore couldn't push it home.

It was a magnificent goal-line stand for the Giants. Earlier they found that hulking Rosy Grier was just too banged-up to be his usual awesome line mainstay—but they readjusted their front line to compensate. Three times the formidable Ameche lunged for the line, and once Unitas took it himself on a sneak. Nothing worked. The Giants were impenetrable.

(Colt Coach Weeb Ewbank felt that the footing at this end of the field was mushy—and the Colts subsequently lost the flip of the coin for the overtime, he chose to defend that same goal, despite the wind, to make sure that his chargers would have good traction. And in later sudden death, Ameche banged in.)

Baltimore had gotten to the 1. On fourth down Ameche took a wide pitchout but Cliff Livingston slashed through the defenses to whip him back to the 5 before he could get started. That ended the thrust.

Had Baltimore scored, it would have "blown the game wide open" in Ewbank's words—but it didn't. A field goal could have made it 17-3 and made it necessary for New York to score 2

18

touchdowns, but the Colts instead went for broke—and "broke" themselves.

And then the game changed. Instantly, astonishingly.

Baltimore had been about to ice it. Then Gifford stung the middle for 5 to get the Giants out of disaster territory, and Webster got 3 more. What did the Giants do then? Conerly dropped back, cocked, and flung a long pass to Rote who took it to the Baltimore 25 before bobbling it. Webster, who was bothered by a bad knee, scooped up the ball and somehow trundled it to the Colt 1. A fantastic play. One moment Baltimore was threatening, the next it was New York. In all, the play swapped 86 yards and obviously shook up the then-dominant Colts. Mel Triplett eventually took it in from the 15 and with Summerall's placement it was 14-10 and a new ball game.

New York swept ahead early in the final period. Conerly hit Schnelker on a 46-yard pass to the Colt 15. Conerly immediately threw to Gifford producing a TD in bang-bang fashion. Just like that it was 17-14, and not only a ball game but a Giant lead.

The Colts didn't panic, though. Unitas went about his business, moved his ball team, and tried for a field goal from the 38 which Bert Rechichar couldn't quite carry.

They got another chance when Phil King's fumble permitted a short advance to the 27—but here the Giants rose up to throw back Baltimore as previously noted, a punt was forced, and New York got the ball. Had the Giants been able to produce a first down, they unquestionably would have won the ball game. But Baltimore stifled the chance, forced the punt, and went on to tie it up in that magnificent final drive.

It was a day for looking up the record books. For Berry it was a great game. His 12 receptions cracked two NFL playoff records—both for catches and for yards (178), both previously held by Dante Lavelli of Cleveland in 1950. Two other records were set: The Giants' 6 fumbles (4 recovered by Baltimore); and rookie Ray Brown's 51-average on 4 punts knocked out Bob Waterfield's LA mark of '50. Just missing records, despite his virtuoso performance, was Unitas. His 26-for-40 was one short of Philadelphia's Tommy Thompson's 27 completions in 1947; and his 349 yards were just 13 shy of Washington's Sammy Baugh's total two decades ago. Ameche was the game's leading rusher with his 65 yards. Baltimore, in general, dominated the statistics. It had much more yardage (460 to 266) and more first downs (27 to 10)—and those 27 were a record by 5.

Baltimore had earned its title shot relatively easily, winning it by the tenth game—whereas New York had to really scramble and actually had to win its last 4 games (the last against formidable Cleveland). New York beat the Browns 13-10 in mid-December to force a playoff which they won 10-0 to take the title. To beat the Browns in that decider, Summerall drilled a field goal from the 49 in a fierce snowstorm that still has people questioning it.

The Scoring:

Baltimore	0	14	0	3	6	—	23
New York	3	0	7	7	0	—	17

NY—FG Summerall 36
Ba.—Ameche 2 (Myhra kick)
Ba.—Berry 15, Unitas pass (Myhra kick)
NY—Triplett 1 (Summerall kick)
NY—Gifford 15, Conerly pass (Summerall kick)
Ba.—FG Myhra 20
Ba.—Ameche 1

The Statistics:

	Ba.	NY
First downs	27	10
Rushing yardage	135	88
Passing yardage	322	178
Passes	26-40	12-18
Own passes intercepted	1	0
Punting	4-51	4-48
Fumbles lost	2	4
Penalties	62	52

20

III

CHICAGO BEARS VS. WASHINGTON REDSKINS
(Game played December 8, 1940)

WASHINGTON, D.C. (Dec. 9, 1940)—Seeing is supposed to be believing, but the 36,034 spectators in Griffith Stadium could hardly be blamed for not believing what they saw here on Sunday. They had come in expectation of seeing a close, hard game of football for the championship of the National Football League.

What they saw was a shambles. What they saw was a magnificently prepared Chicago Bears team thrash the Washington Redskins by the nearly unbelievable score of 73-0. It was a day of rare perfection for the Monsters of the Midway; of humiliating disaster for the Redskins.

The most astonishing thing about the game is not the sheer immensity of the score; it is that such a score could be run up in a pairing of two divisional champions of supposedly well-matched excellence—and that of the two, Washington had been the favorite. The Redskins had the superior record (9-2 in the East, as against Chicago's 8-3 Western slate), and they also had a 7-3 victory over these same Bears just 3 weeks before. The Redskins were 7-to-5 favorites going into the game. Favorites have been upset before, but surely never by so crushing a margin.

By the time the carnage was over, the fantastic Bears had scored 11 touchdowns—and 10 different men had scored them. In all, 15 men had participated in the scoring, including the extra points. Counting running and passing plays from scrimmage and runbacks on kicks and pass interceptions (an amazing 8), the Bears accumulated nearly 700 yards during the sunny afternoon. All 33 Chicagoans played, reserves as well as the regulars—in fact, starting quarterback Sid Luckman played only the first half.

It was, in short, a rout, and the perfect illustration that nothing is ever certain in sports.

Yet those close to the Bear camp were not entirely shocked at what happened. The team's pregame preparation had been more thorough than perhaps for any other game of football yet played. There was a distinct electricity about the team from the final day of the regular season until Sunday's "moment of truth." As Luckman said, "There was a feeling of tension on the club like nothing I've ever experienced before; you felt something tremendous was about to happen." And something tremendous did happen.

But the Bears' confidence was in the face of their earlier defeat by Washington. The Redskins, too, felt sure that they would again whip Chicago on Sunday. The Redskin victory of last month, however, probably was the key factor that made the Bears NFL champions of the 1940 season. It made them mad—and it made them determined.

There were three things in particular about that November game that the Bears remembered vividly right up to Sunday's kickoff: 1.) they felt they should have won and actually were "jobbed." 2.) Washington papers had sneeringly referred to them as "crybabies" for carping about officiating calls. And 3.) Washington owner George Preston Marshall had not only termed them a clutchless "first-half ball club" but proclaimed the Eastern division as having the concentration of league strength. The Bears remembered these things—and indeed, were constantly reminded of them by owner-coach George Halas right up to game time on Sunday. He never let them forget that defeat and what was said afterwards.

What had happened in that 7-3 defeat was essentially this: With less than a minute to play, sub quarterback Bob Snyder hit George McAfee on an improvised long pass good for 49 yards to the 1-yard line. But the Bears had to call time-out to regroup, and since they had used all their time-outs, it cost them 5 yards back to the six. (McAfee pretended to be hurt on the play, but to no avail.) One pass went incomplete, and the second to big Bill Osmanski as the game ended went incomplete also. "Bull" vigorously insisted that his arms had been grabbed on the play and that the Skins should be called for interference. He insisted so vehemently that the Redskins later assailed the Bears as "crybabies"—a headline term that was to backfire on that fateful Sunday.

GAME 1
Green Bay Packers vs.
Dallas Cowboys
December 31, 1967

Boyd Dowler takes a
46-yard pass from Bart
Starr to score for Green
Bay in the second
period. *(U.P.I.)*

Bart Starr, Green Bay quarterback (15), slips through the Dallas line for the winning touchdown. The crucial play came on the fourth down from the 1-foot line with only 13 seconds remaining on the clock. *(U.P.I.)*

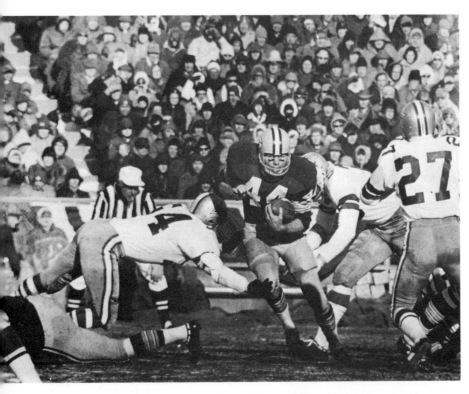

Donny Anderson shakes off tacklers to go for 8 yards in the third period. *(U.P.I.)*

Dallas quarterback Don Meredith (17) completed 10 passes for a total of 59 yards in the losing cause.

GAME 2
Baltimore Colts vs.
New York Giants
December 28, 1958

Alan "The Horse"
Ameche, buried in a
pile of players, took a
handoff from Johnny
Unitas (19) and crashed
across from the 1-yard
line for the winning
touchdown after 8
minutes and 15 seconds
of the Sudden-Death
period. *(U.P.I.)*

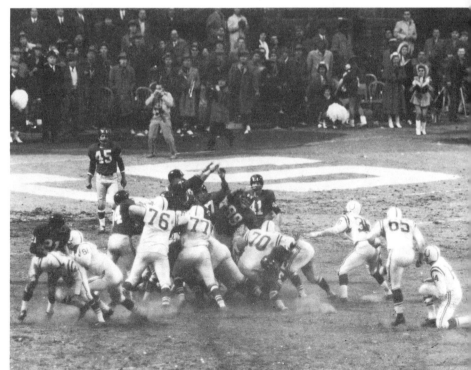

Baltimore's Steve Myhra
(65) kicked the game-
tying field goal from
the 20-yard line in the
fourth quarter. *(U.P.I.)*

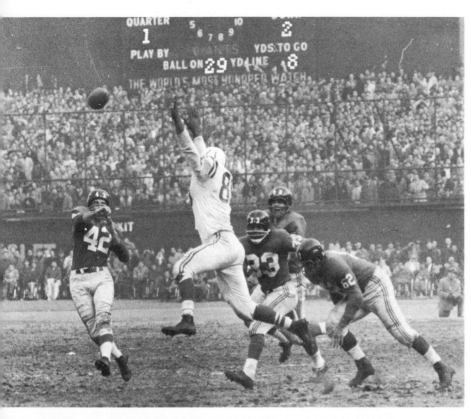

Charlie Conerly, Giant quarterback (42), in action in the first quarter. *(U.P.I.)*

After a Frank Gifford fumble, the loose ball was picked up by Baltimore's Ray Krouse (78) on the Giant 20-yard line. *(U.P.I.)*

GAME 3
Chicago Bears vs.
Washington Redskins
December 8, 1940

Joe Stydahar (13),
Chicago lineman,
gathers in a fumble by
Sammy Baugh (33).
(U.P.I.)

Bill Ozmanski (9)
scored Chicago's first
touchdown in the first
period on a 68-yard
run. *(U.P.I.)*

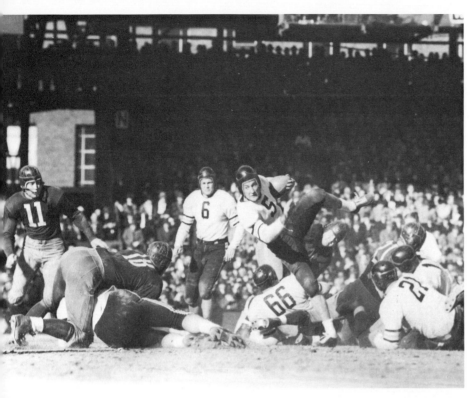

George McAfee (5) of Chicago picks up short yardage. *(U.P.I.)*

Although at times it seemed that Chicago scored every time it took possession of the ball, Bill Ozmanski (9) is brought down by Willie Welker for no gain. *(U.P.I.)*

The Bear players were irate . . . and so was Halas. And Halas did something about it. He posted the Washington clippings on the Wrigley Field bulletin board. He also sought the advice of Clark Shaughnessy, the Stanford University coach who is one of the originators of the T-formation. He and his staff—and players—spent hour after hour poring over the motion pictures of the Redskin game.

They threw out all the plays that had not gained consistently, deciding to stick with those that did gain—and improvised variations on them. The players could not help but benefit from the replays of those losing minutes, watching each man's moves intently. Actually, the Bears didn't drastically change their basic attack—or their defense at all. "The big thing turned out to be the counter-play series," said end Hampton Pool, "but we'd used the counter before—it's just that we found out in studying pictures that the counter worked especially well against the varied Redskin defenses so we put in more counters."

Shaughnessy (he, Halas, and Ralph Jones had been the inventive geniuses of the "T") contributed immensely to the preparations. He also contributed directly before the game. As Bulldog Turner said: "We were a pretty tense bunch of ball players before the kickoff," but Shaughnessy talked to the nerve-tight club and convinced them that they would win, and "somehow we believed him and we went out on the field relaxed" . . . and won.

No team, however, could anticipate such a win.

By the flip of the coin, the Bears had the choice to do what they wanted—receive. Ray Nolting ran the kickoff back from the 2 to his 22, and now Chicago would see how the game developed. (In the dressing room before the game, the coaching staff had set up an early sequence designed to score in 2 or 3 plays—depending on how Washington's defenses were set up.)

The first play was an exploratory slash inside left tackle for 8 yards. More important than the yards gained, the play told the Bears that Washington Coach Ray Flaherty was using the same defense that had worked so well in the previous game against the man-in-motion "T": The linebackers or secondary defense men were following the backs swinging out. Same as in that 7-3 game.

This was what the Bears wanted to find out; so now Luckman used the second of those pre-set plays.

Right half McAfee went in motion, Luckman faked to Nolting into the right side of the Bear line. Osmanski feinted a move to his right, and then swung back to take the ball from Luckman and headed for left tackle. But the hole closed, and Osmanski instead swung outside end and took off along the sideline. Blocks took care of the tacklers immediately up, and the big, fast fullback was on his way. Ed Justice and Jimmy Johnston closed in on Osmanski and seemed certain to nail him around the Washington 35. But burly right end George Wilson was angling across the field and blind-sided Johnston so hard that he scattered both backs out of Osmanski's way. Halas after the game called it "the greatest, most vicious block I ever saw."

(Here, too, might be appended another postgame comment. Osmanski and the Wilsons returned to their hotel in the same taxi, and Mrs. Wilson wondered "who threw the block" that cleared Osmanski. Her husband said nothing printable.)

Osmanski roared by for a 62-yard TD. Jack Manders kicked the PAT, and it was 7-0. All in less than a minute.

Still, Washington was by no means dismayed. It had several key injuries (most of its running backs were hurting), but it still had the incomparable Sammy Baugh to throw the ball. But then Max Krause running back the kickoff 62 yards, was smashed down on the Chicago 32, and was out for the rest of the game with a injured knee. His loss decidedly crimped Baugh's options of a running threat with his other backs out. After a dropped end-zone pass Bob Masterson missed a field goal attempt.

It was still a ball game—but now Chicago had the ball again. They marched 80 yards in 17 running plays to another touchdown, Luckman sneaking it home from the 2. A 14-0 ball game after Bob Snyder's placement.

Thereafter it became a rout.

Baugh obviously had to throw now, but the Bears knew it and rushed him hard every time. Luckman ran the eventual punt back to the Washington 42, and took only one more play to run the score to 21-0. The former Columbia QB flipped a shovel-pass to

Joe Maniaci, who took it the rest of the way. This time Phil Martinovich got the added point.

The second quarter wasn't really sensational. The Bears drove to the 16 but fumbled—and Baugh then fired 10 straight passes to his still-undaunted Skins some 63 yards to the Bear 18. But Nolting intercepted the eleventh, and Washington's chance to get back in the ball game was over.

Before the half ended, Luckman threw to end Ken Kavanaugh for a leaping 30-yard catch as he evaded two Redskin defenders, and it was 28-0. Snyder got this extra point.

It was obvious that the game was over, result-wise. But not for the Bears. They had been stung by Marshall's remarks about being a clutchless "first-half" team, and they weren't about to let things go that easily. They went out and literally destroyed Washington in the second half with Luckman staying on the bench and the reserves seeing heavy duty.

When Baugh tried a short flip two plays into the second half, end Hampton Pool diagnosed things perfectly and snatched the ball for a "gift" TD scamper of 19 yards. It was Dick Plasman's turn to make the PAT: 28-0.

Now Washington really had to gamble if it was to have a chance of saving face if not at winning this ball game. With the ball on its own 33, it tried a desperate fourth-down pass that failed, and Chicago had great position. It didn't waste it. Nolting bolted for 10 yards on the first play, then 23 up the middle, faking Baugh out beautifully near the goal line. Another score.

Not long after that, the flashy McAfee intercepted Roy Zimmerman's pass and whisked 34 yards in a display of his breathtaking open-field running, to put the score at 48-0. Joe Stydahar this time tried and made the place-kick.

Before the third quarter was over, the Bears scored again. Still eternally trying, Washington penetrated to the Chicago 16 before being held. When the Skins subsequently found themselves deep in their own territory and passed, Bulldog Turner plucked it off and took advantage of a great block by Pool to chug 21 yards for the eighth Bear touchdown.

Going into the final quarter: Chicago 54, Washington 0. The

Bears obviously had momentum, the Redskins were stricken. Even with "deep subs" in the game, the Bears ran it up. They couldn't help themselves.

A 74-yard drive was capped by a sparkling 44-yard TD scamper by Harry Clark on a double-reverse and a great feint-out of Frank Filchock near the goal line. When Filchock fumbled shortly afterward, the Bears recovered on the Washington 2-yard line and Gary Famiglietti ripped home on a quick-opener. The PAT went to Maniaci on a pass from Solly Sherman.

The Bears scored one more time on a 50-yard drive with Clark busting up the middle for the last yard. He was the only Bear to score 2 touchdowns in the game. A pass failed to convert the extra point, and that is how the game ended.

Why a pass for the PAT? Very simple: There were no more balls left to play with. On each place-kick the ball soared into the stands, where fans delightedly grabbed it for a souvenir. Eventually, only a scrubby practice ball was left—and rather than kick it out of the playing field and be left without a ball, the Redskin management asked the Bears not to kick for the extra point!

At the same time the Washington management was requesting the Bears to "save" the last football, it was also asking the fans to buy tickets for next season—when the score was in the 50s against the Skins! The loudspeaker came out with the incredible announcement that "Season tickets for the Redskin home games next season will go on sale tomorrow" . . . a hilarious appeal, unbelievably ill-timed.

The Bear win was testimony to superlative pregame preparation. Halas and aides Hunk Anderson, Paddy Driscoll, and Luke Johnson had endlessly gone over old Redskin movies and learned which plays worked best. The Bear players had also watched those same movies over and over. Chicago wanted revenge for that earlier defeat . . . and got it. It also demonstrated that the rejuvenated T-formation was a devastating offense, just at the time when so many other teams were switching to single- and double-wing attacks.

So Sunday would go down in football history. But what about this Bear team in the season ahead? This is a team destined to greatness in the '40s. Halas has the horses.

There is Luckman at quarterback—a great one.

In the T's critical fullback slot there are several great ones: Osmanski, Maniaci, and Famiglietti—all capable not only of overpowering line personnel but of busting loose for long gainers. And for halfbacks there are such men as explosive Nolting, flashy rookie McAfee, Ray McLean, and Clark.

And the line too, is loaded with great ones. Husky George Wilson at one end, and rangy Ken Kavanaugh at the other. In between is brute-force by the names of Stydahar, Turner, Danny Fortmann, Lee Artoe, Ed Kolman, and George Musso. Rookie Turner could go on to real stardom—as could McAfee, who ran a kickoff back 93 yards for a touchdown on the first play he ever ran in the NFL—against the champion Green Bay Packers no less.

This is a fine team, bristling with young talent, that whipped a sound Washington squad on Sunday.

Sammy Baugh realistically said after the game, to a reporter asking whether the game might have gone differently had an early pass not been intercepted: "Yeah, it would have been 73 to 7." Baugh and the Redskins know.

1722976

The Scoring:

Chicago	21	7	26	19	—	73
Washington	0	0	0	0	—	0

Chi.—Osmanski 68, run (Manders kick)
Chi.—Luckman 1, run (Snyder kick)
Chi.—Maniaci 42, run (Martinovich kick)
Chi.—Kavanaugh 30, Luckman pass (Snyder kick)
Chi.—Pool 19, interception (Plasman kick)
Chi.—Nolting 23, run (kick failed)
Chi.—McAfee 34, interception (Stydahar kick)
Chi.—Turner 21, interception (kick failed)
Chi.—Clark 44, run (kick failed)
Chi.—Famiglietti 2, run (Sherman to Maniaci pass)
Chi.—Clark 1, run (pass failed)

The Statistics:

	Wash.	Chi.
First downs	17	17
Rushing yardage	22	382
Passing yardage	223	119
Passes	20-51	7-10
Own passes intercepted	8	0
Punting	3-41	2-46
Fumbles lost	0	0
Penalties	70	25

IV

CLEVELAND BROWNS VS. PHILADELPHIA EAGLES
(Game played September 16, 1950)

PHILADELPHIA, Pa., (Sept. 17, 1950)—The game that professional football has been awaiting for several years was played here yesterday—and the 1949 champions of the now defunct All-American Football Conference utterly shocked the reigning best of the National Football League by a stunning 35-10 score.

NFL backers have long been proclaiming the superiority of their well-established organization—and in the Philadelphia Eagles they had their champion of the last 2 years and a presumably worthy representative. AAFC rooters, though, have increasingly contended that their upstart league had been developing strength rapidly and for their standard-bearer they too had the finest available: 4-time champion Cleveland.

The Browns simply demolished the Eagles. It was no contest. Afterward in the winners' dressing room, chagrined NFL Commissioner Bert Bell acknowledged to Cleveland Coach Paul Brown "You have as fine a football team as I've ever seen."

It was a dramatic way for the Browns to begin play as a new member of the reorganized 13-club National Football League—a league that had scornfully refused even to recognize the existence of the fledgling All-American Conference. They convincingly demonstrated to the record crowd of 71,237 jammed into Municipal Stadium—most of them, by far, Eagles fans—that the AAFC was not the pushover league so many believed it to be; at least, not where these Cleveland gridders are concerned. Cleveland not only turned those 70,000 into believers, but many hundreds of thousands of others around the country as well, including some of the most die-hard NFL supporters.

It must be noted, however, that Philadelphia was physically hurting yesterday. Its great running back, Steve Van Buren, one of the National League's all-time greats, was out due to a foot operation. (Just last year, burly No. 15 gained a record 1,146 yards in a dozen games—including an amazing 196 in 31 carries against the Los Angeles Rams on a muddy field—and became the NFL's all-time career rushing leader.) Missing too was stellar halfback Bosh Pritchard, and captain Al Wistert was hardly his usual effective self at tackle because of a bad knee. In fact, the Eagles were minus not only Van Buren but also young Clyde Scott, who would have taken over the spot at left half. Scott suffered a shoulder separation in the second quarter further reducing the Philadelphia attacking potential.

Such injuries reduced the pregame 7-point odds favoring Philadelphia to generally even money by game time. Regardless of the odds, the bookmakers obviously had no conception of what was to happen yesterday.

Both Coaches Brown of the Browns and Greasy Neale of the Eagles were acutely aware of the significance of this first game between a member of the 31-year-old National Football League and the short-lived (4 years) All-American Football Conference.

It was the Browns who got the jump on their haughtily confident foes. And they kept stomping on them.

Actually, the game began inauspiciously for Cleveland. In the first few minutes they scored a touchdown on a 69-yard punt return by rookie Don "Dopey" Phelps, only to have a clipping penalty nullify it. They not only lost the points but also ace place-kicker Lou "The Toe" Groza as well through an arm injury on the play. (Forrest Grigg ably substituted for him by kicking all 5 extra points.)

Midway through the quarter, Philadelphia marched from its 38, with punishing gains by "Smackover" Scott and Frank Ziegler doing the bulk of the work, before being halted on the Brown 9-yard line (where Tommy Thompson had passes batted away 3 times). Cliff Patton then booted a field goal from the 15 for 3-0. That was the last time the Eagles were in the ball game.

Barely 5 minutes later Cleveland had a touchdown. And it thoroughly wiped the smirks off Philly fans' faces. Otto Graham, the superb ex-Northwestern University quarterback, who had been so brilliant as a pro, started things rolling. By the time the game was over, he had the crowd agog and the Eagles muttering—and the Outstanding Player trophy. His strong right arm threw the ball 38 times, and 21 times he connected for a whopping 346 yards and 3 touchdowns. Not only was his aerial artistry extraordinary, but he also flipped a pitchout for a fourth TD and scored a fifth himself on a QB sneak. All this besides handling the team with aplomb and style.

Moreover, Graham did it against a team that had gained a reputation of being particularly outstanding in pass defense. Last night Neale's veteran crew not only didn't bat away many passes, it permitted ends Mac Speedie and Dante Lavelli to get free for repeated completions (mostly buttonhooks) plus just enough of a ground game to produce a bulging 487 offensive yards.

Graham's first TD strike was to rookie Dub Jones, a 59-yarder, with Jones nabbing the ball up the middle and scooting the last 20 yards all by himself. Less than 3 minutes remained in the first quarter.

Still, though, Philadelphia hung tough. The Eagles recovered a fumble and smashed 40 yards to the Cleveland 5. But the closest they could get was the 2-yard line as hulking Marion Motley (known as a pulverizing fullback line-buster but last night doing a more lustrous job on defense) made successive tackles on the line to stop them.

With a minute and a half remaining before intermission, the Browns scored again—this time Graham pitched to Lavelli from the 26. Lavelli made a gorgeous diving catch in the end zone for the payoff. It capped a 71-yard march in 8 plays. It also was "Automatic" Otto's fourth straight completion behind some fabulous pass protection.

With the score 14-3, it was still anybody's ball game, at least in theory. But in practice, Cleveland thereafter romped away. It got another score in the third period, 2 more in the fourth. Right after the second half began, Graham led his Brownies to an 80-yard scoring assault that saw him complete his seventh consecutive strike with an 11-yard gain to Speedie—who needed but a stride to score.

Along about then, Neale decided that his Eagles needed a change of generalship on the field and replaced Thompson with Bill Mackrides. It worked. With Jack Ferrante, Jack Myers, and Pete Pihos nabbing long-gainers, Philadelphia moved for a TD to close things to 21-7. Pihos latched onto a 17-yarder for the score.

Patton booted the PAT, the final point of the game for Philadelphia.

If Cleveland was concerned, it didn't show. The Browns generally controlled the ball—and 3 minutes after the final quarter began, scored again. This time Graham stuck to the ground, almost as if to demonstrate the Browns' overall power; and with the matchless Motley, Jones, and Rex Baumgardner banging away they swiftly swept for another TD. For the points it was Graham sneaking home for a yard out. That ran it to 28-10—and obviously over.

One more time, though, Cleveland stirred itself. And with just 25 seconds left, scored again. Jones set this one up. He took a handoff from Graham and went loping around left end for 57 yards before finally being snagged on the 7. Baumgardner grabbed Graham's pitchout for the final 2 yards making it 35. Thirty-five points. And this against a stalwart defensive squad.

The AAFC obviously had sent a first-rate football machine against the defending champions of the NFL. Notably, Cleveland overwhelmed Philadelphia in the air—346 yards to 118—and that might have been mildly expected. But the Clevelanders also just about matched their hosts on the ground, being just 7 yards shy with their 141. A full-strength Eagles backfield might have gained considerably more yardage, but still the Browns' defensive gang proved to be infinitely more formidable than anticipated.

Victory is a gratifying vindication for the Browns—and the already disbanded All-American Football Conference. Its champion, albeit representing a defunct league, beat the best of the prestigious National Football League. Now the objective of Paul Brown's Browns undoubtedly is to win the NFL crown, not just the season's opening game.

Attempts had been made before to organize a league that could oppose the long-established NFL. At least the AAFC made its presence felt in post-league prestige. The All-American Football Conference had been organized in June 1944, fully set up in September 1944—and in operation by 1945. It was composed of 8 teams: Buffalo, Brooklyn, Los Angeles, Miami, New York, Chicago, San Francisco, and Cleveland—the latter with Arthur McBride as owner and Brown as coach.

Efforts to get together with the National Football League were met with such comments as "Let them get a football" by NFL

Commissioner Elmer Layden—and for 4 vituperative years the two leagues squabbled. Finally, late in 1949, the leagues agreed that their "war" was working mutual hardships and that they must merge. So 6 weeks later, they did (on NFL terms), and the better clubs of the AAFC were absorbed into the NFL.

Cleveland won the first AAFC crown in the 1946 playoff against the New York Yankees. Thereafter it beat the Yankees again in 1947 by 14-3, whomped Buffalo by 49-7, and then San Francisco by 21-7 to make it a 4-year sweep of conference laurels. It won 19 straight until clobbered by San Francisco, 56-28 in the sixth game of the 1949 season. And now, on Sunday, September 16, it has won the biggest game of all—its introduction into the NFL.

The Scoring:

Cleveland	7	7	7	14	—	35
Philadelphia	3	0	0	7	—	10

Phil.—Patton 15, FG
Clev.—Jones 59, Graham pass (Grigg kick)
Clev.—Lavelli 26, Graham pass (Grigg kick)
Clev.—Speedie 11, Graham pass (Grigg kick)
Phil.—Pihes 17, Mackrides pass (Patton kick)
Clev.—Graham 1 (Grigg kick)
Clev.—Baumgardner 2 (Grigg kick)

The Statistics:

	Clev.	Phil.
First downs	23	24
Rushing yardage	141	148
Passing yardage	326	118
Passes	21-38	11-37
Own passes int.	2	3
Fumbles lost	2	2
Penalties	98	45
Punts	5-40	6-40

V

CHICAGO BEARS VS. NEW YORK GIANTS
(Game played December 9, 1934)

NEW YORK, N.Y. (Dec. 10, 1934)—The New York Giants overpowered the mighty and hitherto undefeated Chicago Bears before 35,000 frozen fans yesterday at the Polo Grounds, scoring 27 points in the last quarter to win the National League playoff, the Ed Thorp Memorial Trophy, and the championship of the football world. The score was 30 to 13.

Going into the last period the Giants, to all intents and purposes, were beaten, 13-3. Ken Strong had made a 38-yard field goal toward the end of the first quarter to put the Giants in front. But the Bears' great fullback Bronko Nagurski had rammed his way to a touchdown in the second period, and Jack Manders, the surest-footed kicker in the league, made the extra point and added a field goal from the 17-yard line to hoist the Bears into a half-time lead, 10-3.

The third quarter was almost over when Manders made another field goal, this one from the 22-yard line. It looked as if the Giants were licked, and the Bears would go through their thirty-second game without a defeat.

But, all of a sudden, as if they had been injected with an explosive, the Giants blasted the Bears out of the lead and buried them under an avalanche of touchdowns. The chilled crowd went wild with joy.

Maybe the basketball shoes that the Giant backs donned between halves had something to do with it. They made 4 touchdowns and 3 extra points in the last 15 minutes.

Ken Strong of N.Y.U. and Ed Danowski of Fordham, a rookie replacement for the injured Harry Newman, ran those Bears ragged while the Giants' linemen crushed Chicago's forward wall. Bill Morgan, a tackle from Oregon, played the game of his life for the Giants being taken out near the end of the game—battered, groggy, but gloriously happy. Strong and Danowski took charge of the crusher that leveled the Bears in the last quarter. With Lou Little,

Columbia's coach, sitting in the stands and phoning to the bench, Giant Coach Steve Owens directed a superb game.

It started with a 35-yard pass from Danowski, which Ike Frankian stole right out of Carl Brumbaugh's intercepting hands in a leaping play on the Bear's goal line, that made the score 13-10, with Strong's conversion.

Minutes later Strong plunged and fought his way for 42 yards and a touchdown, to put the Giants in front, 17-13.

The crowd was on its feet pleading with the Giants to "hold 'em" during the following series. Hold 'em, they did. They stopped the great Nagurski's savage charges, prevented a first down, and took the ball on their own 47-yard line.

From there, with irresistible power, the Giants went to another touchdown. Strong made 2 first downs. Danowski, skirting wide around the Bear's left end, made another. Strong knifed his way through the left tackle to score again. This time the try for the extra point failed as Bo Molenda, who was holding the ball for Strong, fumbled it, whirled and tried a drop kick, which was blocked. The Giants' lead was increased to 23-13.

It was as if the Giants were wound up and Bears were running down. With less than 5 minutes to play, the Giants scored again. Molenda intercepted a pass on the Bears' 32-yard line, flipped a lateral to Dale Burnett who ran it to the 21-yard line. In this last scoring attack, Danowski tore through the Bears 4 times. He scored on a 9-yard run on which he started around the Bears' left end and then cut sharply off tackle, carrying a man with him over the goal line. The extra point was made by Molenda.

With the score 30-13 and only a little time left to play, the Bears made their last desperate effort. Keith Molesworth turned loose a long pass. But the Giants, still on their toes, still playing as if they were behind instead of ahead, intercepted it. Danowski grabbed the ball on the run and threw a lateral again to Burnett, who was on his way to another touchdown when the Bears brought him down between the 10- and 15-yard lines as the final whistle blew.

It was a whirlwind finish in which Strong, the most versatile back in the league, collected 14 points for a total of 17. Danowski, a first-year man, played like a veteran keeping the Bears forever off-balance with his running and passing.

It's no small achievement to score 27 points in 1 quarter against the mighty Bears. In fact, it's a major accomplishment to score enough points to win. No team has defeated them since November 1933, when the Giants turned the trick, 3-0. The Bears were the only undefeated and untied team in the league this year.

The action was comparatively mild at the beginning of the game. The frosty ground hard. The Giants' backs slipped, slid, and fell. Even so, things began to happen almost immediately.

In the first quarter the Giants went 58 yards to the Bears' 7-yard line. Then Link Lyman and Bill Karr threw Danowski for an 8-yard loss, and Gene Ronzani ended the advance by intercepting a Danowski pass in the end zone.

The Bears were working the ball toward midfield when Tex Irwin partly blocked a punt by Molesworth, and Molenda fell on the ball on the Bears' 30. Three plays gained nothing. Strong then kicked a 38-yard field goal. From then until the start of the final period, the constant Bears attack kept the Giants on the defensive.

The second quarter was still young when the Bears obliterated the Giants' 3-point lead. Molesworth returned a punt 20 yards to the Giants' 36. From there they started a series of charges that resulted in a touchdown. A long pass from Molesworth to Ronzani, which slipped out of Flaherty's intercepting hands, took the Bears from the 24-yard line to the 2. The Bears gave the ball to Nagurski, the battering ram. Nagurski lowered his head and charged, taking the ball and a few tacklers with him for the touchdown. Then Manders came in and booted the extra point.

Manders' kicking was one of the notable things about the period. He took 3 shots at field goals, made 1 from the 17-yard line, and missed 2. It was the first time this season that he had missed 2 attempts in the same game.

The Giants had their hands full holding the Bears in the second period. Strong was injured and had to leave the game for awhile. Nagurski went on knocking people down and making yardage.

The last thing Strong did before he was hurt was to fumble a kickoff following Manders' field goal. Karr recovered for the

Bears, and the Giants spent the remainder of the period warding off one assault after another on their goal line. Once Nagurski went over, but a penalty nullified the TD.

But the Giants weathered the storm. They flung themselves on Nagurski; they knocked down Molesworth's passes, and they had the great fortune of Manders' 2 missed field goals.

When they came out for the second half, 10 points behind, the Giant backs wore rubber-soled basketball shoes. A number of their plays had gone askew because the men were unable to keep their footing on the frozen ground. But the effect of the shoes was not particularly noticeable until the last quarter.

Meanwhile, Nagurski, 230 pounds of bone and muscle, continued plowing through the Giants and around them. Every time the Giants brought Nagurski down, he got up more slowly. His constantly hard running was taking its toll. At that point, too, his left arm was injured and almost useless.

But it was a poor pass from Mel Hein to Strong that paved the way for the Bears' fourth shot at a field goal. Manders made this one from the 22-yard line. All told, he made 7 points with his toes.

The score was 13-3, and the third period was almost over when the Giants came to life. Danowski and Strong, with the help of a rejuvenated line, began tearing the Bears to pieces. Danowski hurled 3 straight passes, 2 to Flaherty and 1 to Strong, to put the Giants on the Bears' 30-yard line as the third period ended.

From then on, the Giants swarmed all over the Bears. Strong and Danowski acted as if they had just started to play. The line, which had taken a heavy thumping all afternoon, somehow found the strength to beat down the opposition. The Giants beat the Bears into submission and walked all over them.

The Giants, with this victory in the championship game, avenged two setbacks at the hands of the Bears during the regular league season.

CHICAGO BEARS VS. NEW YORK GIANTS, 1934

The Scoring:

New York	3	0	0	27	—	30
Chicago	0	10	3	0	—	13

Touchdowns: (Giants) Strong (2), Frankian, Danowski (Bears) Nagurski

Field Goals: (Giants) Strong (Bears) Manders (2)

Points After Touchdown: (Giants) Strong (2), Molenda (Bears) Manders

Individual Statistics

N.Y. — FG Strong 38
Chi. — Nagurski 2 run (Manders kick)
Chi. — FG Manders 17
Chi. — FG Manders 22
N.Y. — Frankian 1, interception of Donowski pass (strong kick)
N.Y. — Strong 42, run (strong kick)
N.Y. — Strong — , run
N.Y. — Danowski 9, run (Molenda kick)

VI

NEW YORK JETS VS. BALTIMORE COLTS
(Game played January 12, 1969)

MIAMI, FLA. (Jan. 13, 1969)—National Football League prestige, much as Humpty Dumpty, took a great and embarrassing fall here yesterday. The shove was made by audacious Joe Namath and the New York Jets.

Humbled twice before in the first two Super Bowl games when the awesomely efficient Green Bay Packers demolished their challengers by decisive scores (35-10 over Kansas City, then 33-14 over Oakland), the American Football League yesterday sent its Jets against the Baltimore Colts with few knowledgeable followers giving the Gotham team any chance of upsetting its formidable foe.

But upset the Colts the Jets did—and by the startling score of 16-7. Any margin would have been astonishing. Just the fact that New York won at all made it a most fantastic accomplishment. Those who dote on comparisons might well liken it to David stunning Goliath, Joe Duffer beating Arnold Palmer, Bob Cousy outdunking Wilt Chamberlain. The sort of thing: unbelievable.

But whip the Colts the Jets did. And so today the much-belittled teams of the American Football League can now look the haughty NFLers in the eye without humility. That's what the Jet triumph did: It was more than a game between two teams, "Super" though it was; it was a quest for equality. And as disbelieving NFL players and rooters looked on—75,377 in the Orange Bowl and millions on television—equality is what the AFL earned.

Baltimore may not have been the imposing force of the Green Bay Packers, but it came into the Super Bowl with authentic NFL credentials. It had won 15 times with only a single loss and had overwhelmed Cleveland 34-0 in the league championship playoff—its fourth shutout of the season. The Colt defense was tremendous. And while it was without veteran super-star Johnny Unitas in a starting role owing to season-long injuries, it had a proven quarterback in Earl Morrall who had shown unexpected ability at moving the team in his difficult job of replacing the peerless Unitas. So the Colts were, for real, a fine football team honed in the week-after-week rigors of tough NFL competition.

So what about the upstart Jets? The Jets today were a team driven by destiny—and by a quarterback with ultra sangfroid: Joe Namath. The Jets scored only 1 touchdown, but they also got 3 field goals. It wasn't until the outcome was decided that Baltimore finally got on the scoreboard and then with a solitary touchdown. New York, in short, did today exactly what it set out to do.

It was Joe Namath who did it. He was the catalyst, the inspirational force. Having seen their previous league standard-bearers soundly drubbed in the earlier Super Bowls, the Jets might well have gone into this contest with a fatalistic attitude; for they could not help but read the stories and hear the newscasts constantly proclaiming Baltimore's superiority. (The odds favored the Colts by around 3 touchdowns—actually, a minimum of 17 points.) But the supremely self-assured Namath convinced the Jets that after 2 ignoble Super Bowl whippings this was another game on another day—and they could and indeed would win. He exuded confidence. He abounded in verve. He almost singlehandedly got his teammates to thinking positively that *they could win.*

Namath at 24, sleepy-eyed and long-haired with a well-publicized love for partying, is the prime example of the new athlete of today. Cocksure, vain, a "swinger," and utterly his own man, he may grate on those who prefer their athletic heroes in the old style—but he is a football player who can produce (and who knows it). He produced in high school, he produced in college, he is now producing in the pros.

And his teammates know it. "What we like about him is that he's a winner; he doesn't know about losing" is the way Coach Weeb Ewbank put it. The way tackle Dave Herman put it was "He said we were going to win for sure and we won—he didn't lie, he never lies." It's elementary thinking, but it explains the Jets' outlook.

But for all their optimism, the Jets might well have been blown off the field in the first half. Baltimore almost completely dominated the play. It had its chances: Baltimore whipped the

Jets thoroughly on a solid drive that carried to the New York 20—but didn't score. Baltimore quickly forced a Jet fumble on the 12—but didn't score. Baltimore got a 58-yard run by Tom Matte that penetrated to the New York 16—but didn't score. Had the Colts scored on these early opportunities, the Jets' confidence would probably have sagged beyond reviving—even by a Namath. But the combination of aggravatingly bad luck on crucial plays and the most stubbborn of New York defensing thwarted all of the Baltimore chances.

And New York got better as the game progressed. It ran with power around the middle, it fooled the Baltimore defenders repeatedly, it passed just well enough to make the ground game more effective—and most important, it scored field goals when it couldn't get touchdowns. Further, in getting away without being scored on and then finding they could move the ball, New York perked up mentally: They became more and more convinced that they could win—just as Namath had insisted—and the Jets became increasingly aggressive against Baltimore's frustrated players. At the end the Colts, in desperation, called on the nonpareil Unitas to rally them, but this time the arm-ailing maestro couldn't pull it off—although he did muster a late threat and scored. Too late.

Baltimore came out of the dressing room down 7-0 and grimly intent on taking the fight to the Jets. At this point the Colts were still certain of ultimate victory and felt that if they could start the second half with authority they would put the brash AFL squad on the run. Instead, things immediately went wrong. In a 16-7 game there probably is no one key play, but the first scrimmage play of the second half looms as a particularly vital one. Ewbank himself cites it as the turning point.

Starting out on the 25 after the kickoff, big Tom Matte (who gained 116 yards in 11 carries for a brilliant 10.5 average) smashed ahead for 9 yards—but fumbled. New York linebacker Ralph Baker eagerly pounced on it on the 33. The Jets quickly racked up 2 first downs to the 11 in just 5 plays.

Here the Colts stiffened. Lenny Lyles dragged down Emerson Boozer for a loss at the 16, then hulking Bubba Smith hurled his 295 pounds of 6-foot-7 power into Namath for a 9 yard loss. Namath got his next pass off; but Jerry Logan broke it up, and it was fourth down on the 25. Whereupon Jim Turner booted a field goal from the 32 and the Jets had an exhilarating 10-0 lead. Now Baltimore emphatically needed a lift but did absolutely nothing in 3 plays and had to punt. Taking over on the New York 32, Namath slickly guided his team to a first down on Baltimore's 24 in just 7 plays (6 of them passes, 4 complete). When this drive stalled on the 23, Turner booted his second field goal of the game, making it 13-0.

Four minutes remained in the third quarter when Baltimore coach Don Shula summoned Unitas to go in for the ineffective Morrall. Unable to throw long with his elbow injury—and with New York well aware of it—Unitas had to throw short pitches (lacking their usual zip) and after 3 plays again had to punt. This time the Jets took possession on their 37.

Five plays later New York was down deep on the Colt 6. The big gainer was a 39-yard pass to favorite target left end George Sauer. Namath now stuck to the ground to kill time, knowing that a field goal would be enough to put the game on ice. They worked it to the 2 where Turner kicked his third and final field goal of the game.

That was the ball game. New York now held a comfortable 16-0 lead, and while only 4 plays and a minute and a half had gone by in the final quarter, it was firmly in command. Only improbable heroics could beat them now.

Still, though, there was always the chance (there always is with Unitas on the field, bad elbow or not) that Baltimore could catch fire and pull it out. The next time the Colts got the ball they moved briskly to the New York 25, but Unitas' pass to Jimmy Orr was intercepted in the end zone by Randy Beverly and the first chance was over.

Still sticking to the ground, New York used up almost 5 minutes and managed to get to the Baltimore 35 from where Turner missed a long field-goal try from the 42.

The Colts had their second chance of the quarter. This time they took advantage of it. Taking over on their 20, Unitas threw 7 straight times. (He had attempted only 23 passes during the entire regular season!) He missed his first 3, then desperately fired a fourth time and completed it to Orr for 17 yards. Two more went incomplete before he once again connected, this time to John Mackey for 11—and when the Jets were tagged with a personal foul on the play the ball wound up on the New York 37.

Eight plays later, mostly on 2 good passing gains to Willie Richardson and Orr for 21 and 11, Jerry Hill shot over left tackle for the final yard. Lou Michaels kicked the PAT and it was 16-7. Just 3 minutes and 19 seconds remained to play—not enough.

Baltimore had to get possession immediately—and did. When Tom Mitchell fell on Michaels' on-side kick on the Jet 44, they were in position to go for more quick points. But after Unitas' first 3 short passes clicked, the next 3 failed, and New York took over on its 19. It was as good as over.

It had been over for Baltimore long before—in effect after its early failures to score in that dominant first half. Those missed chances and New York's touchdown now rate examination, but first, consider the teams' pregame plans.

Offensively both were cautious. Without Unitas to throw fear into the opposition, Baltimore's Shula wisely concentrated on a basic running game during the season, using the pass as an auxiliary weapon—and it worked. Morrall did an effective job at QB and won Most Valuable Player honors in the NFL, but he was hardly a scintillating passer. With the powerhouse Colt running attack, though, the whole thing was put together beautifully.

Even with the flashy Namath, New York stuck to an uncomplicated pattern with power drives and simple pass patterns of hooks and flares. During the season the Jets had "shot the works" aerially—but for this game they went conservative. Execution was the thing today, the Jets ramming fullback slants regularly to the left with a change in assignments.

Defensively, Baltimore had had phenomenal success with its shifting zone defense coupled with an 8-man blitz—probably the ultimate in paralyzing opponents' attacks. Against such a maximum charge few quarterbacks were able to stand (or scramble) for long, much less pierce the zone for hits. That ferocious rush crippled every attack it faced during the regular season.

So the Colt blitz was its defensive forte and its strength. So what did Ewbank of the Jets think? "I hoped they would use it—we were ready for it!" And the key man in the Jet attack,

Namath, elaborates: "Any time that safety comes up, that's our key in reading the blitz. After a couple of years together Sauer and I have an automatic going on that situation. We don't call it in the huddle; when the safety blitzes Sauer breaks inside. The time I hit him deep to the outside we'd agreed on the next Colt blitz he would fake in and then fly." Actually, Namath kept the Colts somewhat off-balance by sticking largely to basic ground plays— and when he did throw, it was nothing fancy. The Colts kept expecting him to "do his thing," defensed accordingly, and wound up being whipped by a well-conceived conservatively-based game plan. Two men in particular were the warheads of Broadway Joe's arsenal: fullback Matt Snell and left end George Sauer.

In particular, the Jets concentrated on sending Snell into the line on a weak-side slant. He kept banging away to wind up with 121 yards in 30 carries (besides another 40 on 4 pass catches). It was basic stuff and it worked. Making it work were chief blockers Bob Talamini at guard, Winston Hill at tackle, and path-clearing Boozer at halfback. Sauer latched onto 8 passes for a hefty 133 yards. (Surprisingly, the Jets' other wide receiver, Don Maynard, made nary a catch!) And while Namath's overhead statistics are not especially spectacular, his 17 out of 28 netted 206 yards. Most significantly he did not have an interception in the face of that vaunted Baltimore rush. (Twice in season games astonishingly he was intercepted 10 times!)

As for Baltimore, it had a wretched day offensively, except for Matte's solid line-smashing for 116 yards. Morrall was a meek 6 for 17 and 71 yards, Unitas 11 for 24 and 110. Of course, many of those late Unitas connections came when the confident Jets could afford to "give him" the short ones while guarding against the bomb—a bomb he could hardly wing with his aching elbow (remember, he threw only 23 times during the regular season). And, moreover, Baltimore had 4 pass interceptions along with a most demoralizing fumble.

But enough of game plans and "stix"; consider what happened in that Colt-frustrating and Jet-vitalizing first half. After stopping New York on the first scrimmage of the game, Baltimore moved just as everyone (other than Jet boosters) assumed it would. It swept from its own 27 upfield in a devastating drive that produced

54

3 first downs in just 5 plays, got a fourth in 3 more plays (the payoff on a neat Morrall-to-Mitchell pass for 15 yards), and found itself on the New York 19 with "no sweat."

But here Richardson dropped a pass, another was overthrown, and on the third play Morrall couldn't find a receiver and was stopped at the line. Then Lou Michaels missed a field goal from the 27.

Just before the quarter ended, Baltimore had its second opportunity (set up by a tremendous 51-yard punt by Dave Lee that rolled dead on the 4-yard line. When Lenny Lyles hit Sauer right after catching a pass, the ball bounced loose and linebacker Ron Porter plopped on it at the New York 12. But 3 plays later, with the ball on the 6, Morrall's pass lucklessly bounced high in the air off receiver Tom Mitchell and cornerback Beverly (who had been out-slicked on the play) grabbed it for an interception. Had the pass just fallen harmlessly to the ground, it would have been an almost certain Colt 3-point situation—but instead it was another zero.

New York then put on its scoring drive, turning the game around. First Namath shot Snell into the line for 4 plays to advance from the 20 to the 46 in startling style. He then threw the ball 4 straight times to further advance to the Baltimore 23 with 3 completions. A big play was Sauer's snatch for 14 yards with third and 4 on the Colt 48. From there, Boozer banged for 2, Snell took a pass for a dozen more, and then Snell slammed twice for the touchdown—5 off right tackle and 4 sweeping left.

Babe Parilli came in to hold for the PAT, Turner booted it, and it was 7-0 after just 5:57 in the second quarter.

Baltimore's next muffed chance came after a brief drive to the New York 38 after the kickoff, the big play being a 30-yard Morrall-to-Matte pass. Two plays did little. Cornerback Johnny Sample then broke up a third-down pass, and Michaels tried a field goal from the 46 and again missed.

Now New York moved the ball, getting to the Baltimore 34 before being halted. This time Turner missed a 41-yard field-goal attempt.

Barely a minute later, Baltimore threatened again. This time it was one great run by Matte that did it. The burly back broke free around right end and scooted 58 yards to the New York 16 before finally being nailed. But 2 plays later New York thwarted the threat, the rapacious Johnny Sample coming up to spear the ball for an interception on the 2.

And Baltimore had still another chance before the half ended. It took over on the Jet 42 after the punt and then gambled on a flea-flicker on its second play—and last of the half. Morrall got the snap, handed off to Matte, who then flipped it back to Morrall again. While this was going on, primary receiver Jimmy Orr had gotten free of his man and was hovering around the end zone for a sure 6 points with nobody around him. But Morrall didn't see him! Instead, Morrall threw the ball to Jerry Hill in heavy up-the-middle traffic—and Jim Hudson wound up with the interception.

As Morrall said in the locker room later, "I never saw Jimmy, or else I'd have thrown him the ball." The probable explanation for his failure to spot the completely clear Orr is that a crowd had gathered along the sidelines with the half running out and the confused background made his uniform blend in. Had Morrall seen him, had he hit on the simple pass, it could have been a different ball game.

That's the way the first half went—and the second, as recounted, was the half of decision.

The Jets of course were a jubilant team in the locker room afterwards—many gloating over their stunning triumph over an NFL team, all extremely happy with their victory. For instance: Johnny Sample, the Jet cornerback, defensive captain and ex-Colt, exulted that "I feel pretty good—I've been thinking about this game for three years, every day!" Defense Coach Walt Michaels felt that execution was a major item in the win, especially by the safety men and linebackers (the latter helped out on pass protection). Defensive tackle John Elliott felt that the defensive backs "played one helluva game." And as an offensive man, Snell lauded "the offensive line with its straight-ahead blocking." Ultimately, probably, it was the defensive unit that was mostly responsible for the win. As Ewbank said, "when the defense had to come through it did—and with the big play."

Ewbank unquestionably came up with a magnificent game

56

plan—and one no doubt based on his knowledge of the Colts from his days as their coach. And his victory must have been sweet indeed after having been fired by Baltimore 6 years ago after 9 years of working with the team. He even piloted the Colts to an NFL title in 1958. He subsequently picked up numerous Colt castoffs for his Jets, a fact which he made much of in his pregame talk in reminding his squad that most of them were NFL "nothings."

Ewbank also conceivably knew that ace defensive end Ordell Braase of the Colts was not at his best—and that is where much of the Jet attack was directed (giving Braase and linebacker Don Shinnick a rough time). Tackle Winston Hill acknowledged that "Braase is too good a football player to have me drive him off the field—he had to be hurt or something." Not only was Braase off form but a remarkable number of Colts wound up being banged-up in the game: Fred Miller, Rick Volk, Bob Vogel, and Braase all left the field for one reason or another—and this on a team which has had remarkable durability.

For whatever reasons, the Jets wound up with $15,000 apiece and the Colts with $7,500. They and the American Football League wound up with the championship.

The Scoring:

New York	0	7	6	3	—	16
Baltimore	0	0	0	7	—	7

NY—Snell 4, run (Turner kick)
NY—FG Turner 32
NY—FG Turner 30
NY—FG Turner 9
Ba.—Hill 1, run (Michaels kick)

The Statistics:

	NY	Ba.
First downs	21	18
Rushing yardage	142	143
Passing yardage	195	181
Passes	17-29	17-41
Own passes intercepted	0	4
Punting	4-39	3-44
Fumbles lost	1	1
Penalties	5-28	3-23
Offensive plays (including times thrown)	74	64

Individual Statistics:

Rushing

New York—Snell 30 attempts for 121 yards, Boozer 10 for 19, Mathis 3 for 2.

Baltimore—Matte 11 attempts for 116 yards, Hill 9 for 29, Morrall 2 for minus 2, Unitas 1 for 0.

Passing

New York—Namath 28 attempts for 17 completions and 206 yards, Parilli 1 for 0.

Baltimore—Morrall 17 attempts for 6 completions and 71 yards, Unitas 24 for 11 and 110 yards.

Receiving

New York—Snell 4 completions for 40 yards, Sauer 8 for 133, Mathis 3 for 20, Lammons 2 for 13.

Baltimore—Richardson 6 completions for 58 yards, Mackey 3 for 35, Orr 3 for 42, Hill 2 for 1, Matte 2 for 30, Mitchell 1 for 15.

VII

CLEVELAND BROWNS VS. LOS ANGELES RAMS
(Game played December 24, 1950)

CLEVELAND, OHIO (Dec. 25, 1950)—Lou Groza shrugged off his sideline cape and trotted onto the field in the dusk of Municipal Stadium yesterday responding to the wave-in and call from his Browns teammates waiting there on the icy gridiron near the goal line.

"Groza . . . Groza . . ."

Like the Night Before Christmas, not a person was stirring in the hushed crowd of 29,751 gathered in the frigid bowl—for every one of them and the 2 teams standing grimly on the frozen turf knew that this would be the climactic moment of nearly 60 minutes of bristling offensive football being played for the championship of the National Football League.

Waiting with confidence—and inescapable apprehension—were the Cleveland Browns, ready to line up at the 10-yard line for the field goal that could snatch this 28-27 game from defeat. Waiting, too, were the Los Angeles Rams, bracingly trying to convince each other that they could thwart the kick that was coming—a kick that "The Toe" could hardly miss from squarely in front of the goalposts at that range.

The burly Groza reported in, meticulously stepped off his kicking distance, and Tom James knelt for the ball at the 16-yard line. It flew back, he set it up, and Groza kicked it long and true.

In that dimming light on Christmas Eve, Cleveland won a tumultuous 30-28 last-second victory over the Rams to claim the championship of the National League. Only 20 seconds were left when Groza did his thing—a field goal that not only meant proud possession of the title but $1,113 apiece for the winning Browns. It was a triumph for the Browns to richly savor, proving once again—as they have repeatedly done all season—that their 4-year mastery of the oft-sneered-at, defunct All-American Football Conference was no fluke. They had been admitted to the long-established NFL with the taunt, "Now we'll see how good these AAFC hotshots are; now they'll be playing against *professionals* and not pushovers."

Throughout this long season, with every opponent making their point for them, they had demonstrated their skills, losing but 2 of their dozen games (both to New York) in capturing the All-American-Conference crown and then going on to beat the Giants in a playoff. Now they have proved to all scoffers that they are indeed quite a football team. Professionals.

And they did so in a game that NFL Commissioner Bert Bell later called "the greatest football game I ever saw."

And the game was all of that. The 2 teams played all-out football for all 60 minutes before the 30,000 spectators (who were whipped by intermittent snow flurries driven by a 28 mile-an-hour wind) and the countless thousands of others following the action on radio and television.

The Rams scored first—in fact, in the opening 27 seconds—but Cleveland fought back to tie it up. Then LA scored once more for 17-7 at the end of the first quarter. By half time the Browns had narrowed the difference to 14-13, and early in the third quarter had surged into a 20-14 lead. Before the quarter ended, however, Los Angeles had not only regained the lead but had struck again for a commanding 28-20 advantage. Cleveland needed more than a touchdown to win in the remaining quarter—and got it: 10 points.

There was only 1 minute and 48 seconds left and 68 yards to the distant goal when the Browns got the ball for the last time, trailing by a single point at 28-27. They didn't get all those 68 yards, but they got all but 10 of them to gain position for the winning field goal.

The way they did was a masterpice of quarter-backing by the incomparable Otto Graham; he had to gain huge chunks of yardage against both the Rams and the clock. He did so with the help of Coach Paul Brown masterminding plays from the sidelines.

Graham tried to pass on the first play, couldn't find a free receiver, and ran with the ball himself for 14 yards. Most important, he ran out of bounds and stopped the clock. Next he hit Rex Baumgardner in the left flat for 15 more yards—and Baumgardner, too, was able to run out of bounds. Another pass

60

missed, but then he connected to Dub Jones on the right side, and the young back got to the 22. Once more Graham threw, now trying the left side and again to Baumgardner. Down to the 11—and again out of bounds to gain precious time.

Forty seconds were left.

Graham looked at the clock, decided that putting the ball into the air was too dangerous, and sagely took it himself on a sprint to the middle of the field. His intention was to gain position rather than yardage, but he managed to get to the 10 before being dropped. He had the position he wanted.

It was only second down, but the Browns had supreme confidence in The Toe (he had kicked a record 13 field goals during the regular season, 2 more in last week's 8-3 divisional playoff win over the New York Giants). So Graham waved to the bench: "Groza!" The Stadium hushed as Lou trotted out. In the back of everyone's mind was the remembrance of an earlier kick, when holder Tom James was unable to handle a low snap from center on an extra point and had to try a desperation pass instead of letting Groza kick. A recurrence would be catastrophic.

But this time the snap was perfect, James spotted the ball perfectly, and The Toe swung. There was never a doubt where the pigskin was going once it took off in the dusk.

Still, there was time for the Rams to pull off a miracle finish. After all, hadn't they struck for an 82-yard TD in the first 27 seconds of this improbable game? After Jerry Williams ran the kickoff back to his 47, Bob Waterfield remained on the bench, and Norm Van Brocklin came in at quarterback for the first time in the game. The strong-armed Dutchman hurled the ball far upfield, but Warren Lahr intercepted on the 5 and it was over.

For the spectators, though, the excitement was to continue for a long time; they poured onto the field, mobbing the Cleveland players and uprooting the goalposts in a frenzy of delight.

While the drama focused on the final place-kick, it had been a matchlessly spectacular game all along. As emotionally spent Coach Paul Brown said, wandering about the Brown's locker room congratulating players, "This one will be remembered a long time."

It was Los Angeles that provided the first thrill. It did so on the first play from scrimmage with an electrifying 82-yard pass from Waterfield to fleet Glenn Davis. The former Army star plucked in the ball near midfield and sprinted the rest of the way before the stunned Cleveland crowd. Waterfield's kick made it 7-0 and only 27 seconds had elapsed.

But the Browns themselves were far from dismayed. Six plays after they had taken the kickoff, they too had points. The climax of the 70-yard march was a 31-yard pass from Graham to Jones, and when Groza booted the PAT it was 7-all and just 3:10 had gone by.

Less than 4 minutes later, with the clock stopping at 7:05, the Rams had their lead back in this wild offensive spectacle. To get it, they drove 80 yards in 8 plays, with Dick Hoerner smashing inside right tackle for the last 3 yards. Now 14-7.

It stayed that way until early in the second quarter, when Graham pitched to Dante Lavelli for a 35-yarder at 2:20. But the "automatic" extra point never came off. James had trouble handling the poor snap, and Groza could only stand helplessly while James vainly tried to flip the ball into the end zone: 14-13.

Four minutes after the second half began, though, Cleveland had its lead. Lavelli did it with his second TD catch, this one for 39 yards from Graham. When Groza drilled the PAT home it was a 20-14 ball game.

But 5 minutes later Los Angeles punched 71 yards, with Hoerner capping the 11-play drive by slamming home from a yard out. Waterfield's kick regained the lead for LA at 21-14.

Then disaster struck the Browns. Big Marion Motley was belted by several Rams as he tried to change direction on the frozen sod on the ensuing kickoff—and end Larry Brink scooped up his fumble and sped 7 yards into the end zone. Waterfield added the placement, and it was now a bulging 28-20 margin for the Rams. And the whole thing had taken only 21 seconds.

Those 2 quick touchdowns put Cleveland in deep trouble, even with 5:19 left in the third quarter and the whole fourth remaining to be played. But the rest of the third canto went by without a score, and time increasingly became a factor.

With 4 and a half minutes gone in the last period, Cleveland finally got 7 points closer. Graham nursed the Browns down to the

GAME 4
Cleveland Browns vs.
Philadelphia Eagles
September 16, 1950

Don Phelps (94)
scampers through the
Eagle squad for a first-
period touchdown—
called back on a
clipping penalty.

Mac Speedie is on his way with a pass from Otto Graham. Neill Armstrong (80) of the Eagles moves in for the tackle.

Clyde Scott manages to pick up 10 yards and a first down for the Eagles before he is stopped by Cleveland's defensive back, Warren Lahr.

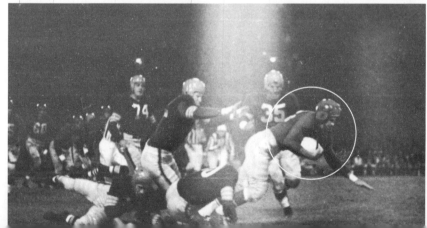

Jack Myers (32) tries to slip away from Cleveland's Tony Adamle and John Kissell after taking a pass from Tommy Thompson.

GAME 5
Chicago Bears vs.
New York Giants
December 9, 1934

Chicago's Carl
Brumbaugh tosses the
ball to Bronko
Nagurski in the first
period.

It took at least 2 Giants
to bring down Bronko
Nagurski. *(U.P.I.)*

Giant quarterback Ed
Danowski donned
basketball shoes at the
start of the second half
—and changed the
course of the game.

GAME 6
New York Jets vs.
Baltimore Colts
January 12, 1969

Matt Snell (41), Jet's
fullback, carries the ball
in the first quarter.
(U.P.I.)

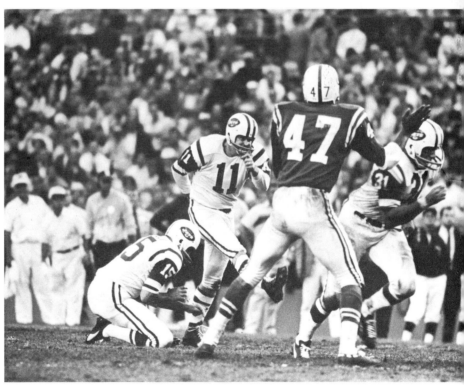

Jim Turner (11), of the
Jets, kicks his first field
goal of the afternoon
with Babe Parilli (15)
holding.
*(Photo by Barton
Silverman)*

Baltimore tight end
John Mackey (88) gets
away from Hudson (22)
only to be brought
down by Al
Atkinson (62). *(U.P.I.)*

Joe Namath (12) hands off the ball to Emerson Boozer. *(U.P.I.)*

Johnny Unitas (19) passes during a third period drive. *(U.P.I.)*

LA 14-yard line, tossed to Baumgardner for the TD, and Groza added the extra point to make it 28-27.

But time continued to tick away—ever working against the Browns. Two punts were exchanged. And then, with 5 minutes left, a Waterfield pass was intercepted by Tom Thompson at midfield and Cleveland had field position. Graham quickly pitched to Jones for 22, and the crowd began roaring "Go . . . go . . ." to its Browns.

But when Graham was hit and fumbled, Milan Lazetich popped on it for the Rams and the threat was killed. Now only 3 minutes were left.

A first down for Los Angeles would do it, insuring ball control for the rest of the playing time—but the determined Cleveland defenders forced Waterfield to punt. He booted it far upfield to Cliff Lewis back on his 14. Lewis ran it back to the 32, and Cleveland was set to begin what everyone knew had to be its last drive. A minute and 28 seconds later it had the 3 points it needed for victory.

It was the sixth straight year that a team from Cleveland won a league championship! The Cleveland Rams won the NFL crown in 1945, then the Browns captured AAFC titles in 1946 through 1949, and now an NFL wreath in 1950.

Illustrative of the flashy offensive show put on by the 2 teams is the fact that 6 playoff records were set and 3 tied. The records:

Longest completed pass play—82 yards by Bob Waterfield to Glenn Davis (Los Angeles), breaking the record of 77 by Sammy Baugh to Wayne Millner (Washington) in 1937.

Longest pass reception—82 yards by Davis.

Most passes caught—11 by Dante Lavelli (Cleveland), breaking the record of 9 by Millner (Washington) and Jim Benton (Cleveland) in 1937 and 1945.

Punting average—50.3 yards by Waterfield (Los Angeles), breaking the record of 49 by Kay Eaken (New York) in 1941.

Total passes by both teams—65, breaking the record of 61 by Washington and Chicago Bears in 1940.

First downs passing—13 by Cleveland, breaking record set by Philadelphia against Chicago Cardinals in 1947.

Tied were these records: 2 touchdown passes to Lavelli,

equaling the mark held by Bill Karr and Dante Magnani of the Bears and Millner of the Redskins; 2 rushing touchdowns by Dick Hoerner, matching Norm Standlee of the Bears; and 4 intercepted passes on Waterfield, tying Arnie Herber's mark for New York.

Both Graham and Waterfield had fine throwing days in spite of the gusty wind and low temperature. Graham completed 22 of 32 passes for 298 yards and 4 touchdowns. Waterfield hit 18 of 31 for 312 yards and 1 TD. He had, however, 4 interceptions. Waterfield, incidentally, barely missed a field goal in the second quarter from almost the identical spot from which Groza kicked his game-winner.

As for Groza's kick, the sweating 235-pound Browns tackle kissed his shoe in the locker room after the game and insisted, "Honestly, I wasn't nervous—not any more than last week" (when his 2 field goals atop a safety beat the Giants 8–3). Seeing New York Yankee relief pitcher Joe Page nearby, he kidded with him, "You never get nervous in a spot like that, do you, Joe?" . . . to which Page bluntly retorted, "The hell you don't!"

Both Coach Brown and defeated Coach Joe Stydahar lauded each team as "magnificent." Brown further praised his own squad as being "the gamest bunch of ball players in the business"—to which Line Coach Ewbank added, "Those Browns just wouldn't say they were licked!"

In the gloomy Rams' dressing room, Waterfield and Joe Stydahar both agreed that "it was just one of those things."

The Scoring:

Los Angeles	14	0	14	0	—	28
Cleveland	7	6	7	10	—	30

LA—Davis 82, Waterfield pass (Waterfield kick)
Clev.—Jones 31, Graham pass (Groza kick)
LA—Hoerner 3, run (Waterfield kick)
Clev.—Lavelli 35, Graham pass (improvised pass fails)
Clev.—Lavelli 39, Graham pass (Groza kick)

CLEVELAND BROWNS VS. LOS ANGELES RAMS, 1950

LA—Hoerner 1, run (Waterfield kick)
LA—Brink 7, fumble return (Waterfield kick)
Clev.—Baumgardner 14, Graham pass (Groza kick)
Clev.—FG Groza 16

The Statistics:

	Clev.	LA
First downs	22	22
Rushing yardage	73	95
Passing yardage	298	312
Passes	22-33	18-32
Own passes intercepted	1	5
Punting	5-38	4-51
Fumbles lost	3	0
Penalties	3-25	4-48

VIII

CHICAGO CARDINALS VS. CHICAGO BEARS
(Game played November 28, 1929)

CHICAGO, ILL. (Nov. 29, 1929)—The Chicago Cardinals out-scored the Chicago Bears here on Thanksgiving Day, 40-6, in snow-draped Comiskey Park.

So did Ernie Nevers. In the most explosive one-man scoring extravaganza in professional football annals—if not in *all* of football history—the great Cardinal fullback-coach went on a personal rampage to pierce the Bear defenses for 6 touchdowns and 4 extra points: all 40 points scored by his team! It is unlikely that any man will ever match his virtuoso performance.

The 8,000 spectators who shivered through the game had come in expectation of seeing both a closely fought and a low-scoring contest. Hadn't the 2 teams battled to a scoreless tie the last time they met earlier in the season? And weren't their records nearly the same—the Bears 4-6-1, the Cardinals 4-5-1? Everything pointed to a repetition of that previous zero-zero meeting.

But this time the incomparable Nevers wouldn't and couldn't be stopped. Nor could the Cardinals. This time the match-up between these two Windy City arch-rivals was a red romp. The Redbirds simply overwhelmed the Bruins. Not even the presence of Harold "Red" Grange in the Bear lineup could alter things. Nor, for that matter, could the out-of-retirement token appearance of legendary Jim Thorpe help the Cardinals.

This game could well go down in football history not because of Nevers, but simply because it featured 3 of the most illustrious names in the game: Nevers . . . Grange . . . Thorpe . . . all men of incontestable stature—all All-Timers, not "just" All-Americans. But Grange was not the Grange of yore when he dazzled opponents with his breakaway running; since a cruel knee injury 2 years ago, he simply was not the runner he once was—although still a fine one. And Thorpe in his 40s, even with his amazing body and talents, could not compete with raw, strong youth. "Old Jim" just could not get his much-punished, muscle-bound sinews to overpower opponents the way he could in his glory years.

So it was Nevers' day. And what a day! The former Stanford back never did set the fans agog with gaudy open-field running, but he did have them marveling at his smashing power and style. He scored 6 times on runs of 20, 4, 6, 1, 1, and 10 yards. All elemental savage bursts.

After missing his first extra-point kick, which was wide, he booted 3, missed the next one because of a bad snap, and then made the final try: 4 of 6.

And—he also blocked for his teammates. Such backs as Mickey McDonald and quarterbacks Gene Rose and Cobb Rooney gained their share of yardage either running or pass-catching—and Nevers' Bear-jarring blocks were frequently key ones. But that great Cardinal line was the main thing in making the score what it was; the Card up-fronters were devastating.

The Cardinals scored the second time they had the ball. Setting up the TD was a lateral from Nevers to McDonald, who broke away for some 30 yards. Then big Duke Slater blasted open a hole off the tackle slot for Nevers to go the rest of the way: 6-0 in barely 6 minutes.

Before the first half ended, Nevers had done it twice more. A pass interception led to the next score by giving the Cardinals the ball on the Bear 29. A few tricky plays, one of them a triple pass, advanced the ball to the 4-yard line, from which Nevers dove home. More fancy stuff helped produce the third TD, a triple reverse being the big gainer—but in the end it was brute power that bulled it in, with Slater charging ahead of Nevers off tackle from the 6. So it was 20-0 for the Cardinals—and Nevers.

A nifty jaunt of nearly 40 yards by Rooney set up the first touchdown of the second half, this time Nevers taking it in from 1 yard out.

Now down 27-0 and with a rout looming, the Bears saved face. Walt Holmer threw the ball to Garland Grange (Red's younger brother), who went wide and eluded Rooney to go all the way for 60 big yards and a score. Northside fans cheered their lungs out here, for what it was worth. When Holmer's kick failed it was

27-6—and, although he subsequently passed the Bears to the Cardinal 30, the Bears would never score again.

Before the game ended, Nevers had scored twice more on vicious chops into the line. He got those last 2 in the first 10 minutes of the final period, then eased off. But before he called it quits, he had indubitably set a record not just for this year but probably for all time. When he left the field, the gleeful Southsiders gave him a tremendous ovation on that cold and snowy Thanksgiving afternoon. He had earned it.

The Cardinals had a chance of finishing ahead of the Bears in the NFL standings, although it is unlikely that they could overtake Green Bay's amazing undefeated Packers for the championship. But licking the Bears is enough.

Great as his performance was, going back over Nevers' career produces many a day of awesome feats.

He began as a youth in Superior, Wisconsin, knowing nothing about the game. But his coach, Irl Tubbs, kept him at it, and he eventually wound up at Stanford to win All-American laurels. In his senior year of 1925, he suffered a broken leg and played less than a quarter of the season; then, when the leg had mended, he broke an anklebone in practice. That was the year Stanford met Notre Dame in the Rose Bowl. So what did Nevers do against Notre Dame in the Rose Bowl? With his cast barely removed, he played the full 60 minutes, carrying the ball 34 times and gaining 114 yards. This against a formidable fighting Irish team.

The ruggedly handsome blond fullback, still short of credits for graduation, then signed with his "home town" Eskimos of Duluth, Minnesota, to pick up some pro money. He was an immediate standout both on the field and as a publicity draw. Duluth played 13 games as a member of the National Football League (it was 6-5-2), but also played 16 more on the exhibition route. During those 29 games, the fantastically durable fullback played 1,713 minutes of a possible 1,740.

And he did everything: He blocked, he ran, he passed, he kicked. His place-kicking was prodigious. In one game against Hartford, for instance, he booted 5 field goals of 42, 21, 28, 26, and 25 yards for an NFL record that will most likely stand for years. Against Pottsville he threw 17 straight completions; and in one game against Milwaukee completed a record 62-yard pass to end Joe Rooney (in a 7-6 victory). As a runner, he was not the breathtaking all-the-way runner who piles up spectacular yardage— but he pounded the line ferociously and was rarely stopped without inflicting punishment, and he broke free often enough to provide those long-range thrills too.

For all his offensive splendor, he did yeoman work on defense—and was proud of it. As an example, late in his rookie year as a pro the Eskimos played New York in the Polo Grounds and, against a team that had held 7 opponents to just 3 touchdowns, fought them to a 14-13 score. Even in the loss, Nevers was outstanding with his tackles, a pass interception, and a stretch of 9 consecutive line plunges to eventually score a TD himself. It was a crescendo performance.

Although figures are uncertain, Nevers reportedly earned in the vicinity of $20,000 for that gruelingly long season.

Despite the fact that the Cardinals began playing long before the Bears, they never quite caught on with Chicago fans nor drew the crowds as large as their Northside rivals—and this despite the presence of brilliant Paddy Driscoll in Cardinal uniform. (Bear owner George Halas tried for years to get Driscoll, but was not successful until 1926.)

Hard-pressed Cardinal owner Pat O'Brien was permitted by league president Joe Carr to sell Driscoll to the Bears to raise money so that the NFL could buck a new pro league set up by the venturesome C. C. Pyle (who had signed up Grange, the greatest star in football). But eventually O'Brien had to sell the team to a Chicago doctor, David Jones, the agreed price coming to $25,000. The new owner immediately signed Nevers as player-coach. So Nevers became a Cardinal. (Oddly enough, when Nevers kicked his 5 place-kicks against Hartford in 1926, he knocked another Cardinal—and the most illustrious one before him—off the record books: Driscoll. Paddy had drop-kicked 4 FGs of from 18 to 50 yards against Columbus the year before. That year, incidentally, saw the Cardinals finish with a 9-2-1 record as against Pottsville's 10-2 . . . but then Chicago scheduled extra 2 games, won them, and beat out Pottsville for the championship!).

78

It might also be noted that it was against the Cardinals that Grange made his official pro debut in 1925, also on a Thanksgiving Day—and wound up with the Bears settling for a scoreless tie. And the man perhaps most responsible was Driscoll, who kept punting the ball either out of bounds or away from the famed former Illinois "Redhead" all afternoon—an accomplishment that drew heated boos from the fans after the game because it had prevented Grange from doing his breakaway specialty, which was what they had come to see.

Although Grange was not "The Grange of Old" because of his knee disability, professional football owes him a debt beyond repayment. More than any other man, he made the game what it is today, just 4 years after his departure from college.

His fabulous exploits at the University of Illinois hardly need retelling. His "No. 77" and "Galloping Ghost" tags are nationally known. From schoolboy fame at Wheaton, Illinois, where he was a track and football star (after gaining both strength and fame as a 140-pound "iceman" by lifting a 75-pound chunk of ice to his shoulder, he became a legend by his junior year with the Illini. In particular, his magic game against Michigan—6 touchdowns accounted for on runs of 95, 67, 56, 45, and 12 yards and an 18-yard pass, in all gaining 402 yards in 21 carries besides his passing—is collegiate football history. That was 1924.

Grange then signed up with C. C. Pyle in an extravagant deal with Halas and the Bears immediately after his final collegiate appearance. After that first pro game with the Cards on Thanksgiving Day 4 years ago, he played a merciless schedule of exhibitions that included a string of 7 games in 10 days. But he made perhaps a quarter of a million dollars.

The next year he and Pyle wound up in New York, and in 1927 they had an NFL franchise. And Grange also had a bad knee, received when his cleats dug in just as he was being smacked by the Bears' George "Brute" Trafton. It was a debilitating, star-destroying injury, and Grange was on crutches for months afterward. He couldn't play at all the next year, but then Halas inveigled him to come back to the game—and he did, despite having to play with a cumbersome steel brace on his knee. Red himself says that "I'm just another halfback now," but this is hardly true—and with his immense football talents and instinct he could become a great defensive back despite losing his breakaway artistry. So Grange played on Sunday, but he was hardly the scintillating star of the last half-dozen years when his name became a household word in America.

As for Thorpe, the great "all-everything" athlete could contribute little toward the Cardinal triumph. The onetime Carlisle star, who became an Olympic legend and a competent performer in every sport he attempted, is simply too old to bash bodies with the young bloods.

In his prime, Thorpe was perhaps without a peer—and in any game, as the 1912 Olympics testify—but yesterday he was just a mite too old. "The Old Injun" was willing, but this so-called comeback was little more than a nostalgic appearance.

So for this trio of All-Time greats, Thorpe is reluctantly out of the game . . . Grange still has his fire but is more likely to become famed for his defensive savvy . . . and Nevers in his iron-man way could go on for years as one of football's nonpareil battlers.

This Thanksgiving Day will be remembered!

The Scoring:

Bears	0	0	6	0	—	6
Cardinals	13	7	7	13	—	40

IX

NEW YORK GIANTS VS. CHICAGO BEARS
(Game played December 17, 1933)

CHICAGO, ILL. (Dec. 18, 1933)—In a sensational shower of forward passes, George Halas' Chicago Bears won the first National Football League championship game here yesterday, beating the New York Giants, 23-21, in a game witnessed by nearly 30,000 at Wrigley Field. Just prior to the season, the league was broken up into two divisions, East and West—the brainchild of George Preston Marshall, owner of the Washington Redskins.

The Bears, trailing 21-16, snatched victory out of the air in the dramatic closing minutes of the game. Billy Karr, right end, took a long lateral pass, eluded 2 Giant tacklers, and galloped 25 yards for the deciding score.

The game was a thrilling combat of forward-passing skill, desperate line plunges, and top gridiron strategy that kept the chilled customers on their feet in constant excitement.

The game was also a revelation for college coaches who advocated no changes in the rules. It was strictly an offensive duel, and the professional rule that allows passes to be thrown anywhere behind the line of scrimmage was responsible for nine-tenths of the thrills.

Chicago's man-in-motion T-formation attack, tailored especially for 235-pound Bronko Nagurski, former University of Minnesota plunging fullback, was too much for the Giants. Nagurski gained 65 yards in 14 attempts and tossed the pass that was responsible for the winning touchdown. Nagurski was ably assisted by "Automatic" Jack Manders, another former Gopher, who kicked 3 field goals—one for 50 yards—missed another attempt, and kicked a point after touchdown for a total of 10 points.

Harry Newman, Michigan's All-American quarterback in 1932, was the outstanding star of the Giants' attack. He tossed 17 passes, completing 12 for a total of 201 yards and 2 touchdowns.

Hailed as the greatest offensive teams in professional football, the rivals did not waste any time in proving it, although the field was sloppy, particularly in the grassy spots, because of mist and fog that hung over the field as the game started.

Keith Molesworth quick-kicked over Newman's head and gave the Bears their first scoring chance. Ken Strong returned the punt to the Giant 42-yard line. There Nagurski plucked a pass out of the air and raced to the Giant 26. Gene Ronzani slashed over right tackle to the 15. Three plays netted 8 more yards, but they had to settle for a field goal by Manders from the 16. The ball sailed squarely between the goalposts.

In the second period Ronzani passed to Molesworth, netting the Bears 17 yards and placing the ball on the Giant 29. The New York team's defense tightened, but Manders, called upon for the second time, booted the ball between the uprights on a 40-yard effort.

The Giants, stirred to desperation, came back with a touchdown, with Morris Badgro taking Newman's pass and running 29 yards. Richards paved the way for the score with a 30-yard drive off left tackle to the Bear 29-yard line. Strong kicked the extra point and the Giants led, 7-6.

The Bears missed another scoring opportunity just before the half ended when Red Grange got away on a 17-yard gallop around left end to the Giant 9. There Manders attempted another field goal, but this time failed.

With both teams fighting desperately and using all the strategy at their command, things began to happen in the third period. No sooner did the Bears get the ball than they went right down the field. Ronzani gained 15 yards on one play; and a pass, Molesworth to Carl Brumbaugh, brought the ball to the Giant 13. Once more the Giants stiffened, but Manders dropped back to the 19-yard line to score with another field goal that gave the Bears the lead, 9-7.

The lead didn't last long, as the Giants, with Newman heaving the ball to Burnett, Richards, and Max Krause, drove down the field for 61 yards in 8 plays and a touchdown, with Krause plunging over from the 1-yard line. Strong kicked the PAT.

Then the Bears took a turn at scoring with amazing speed, and in 6 plays chalked up a touchdown. George Corbett faked a punt and passed to Brumbaugh for 67 yards, which was the spark. It brought the ball to the Giant 8. Nagurski, after two plays, faked a plunge and tossed a pass over the goal line to right end Karr. Manders added the extra point, and the Bears went into the lead again, 16-14.

The Giants struck back on the kickoff. They took the ball on their 26-yard line and, resorting again to the air, brought it to the 8-yard line. There, Newman wound up the spectacular display by tossing a pass to Strong in the end zone. Again Strong added the extra point, and the Giants led, 21-16.

Then came the thrilling climax. The Bears, apparently beaten, took the ball on the Giant 47-yard line after a bad punt. The Bears took to the air. The first pass, Molesworth to Brumbaugh, brought the ball to the Giant 32. The next one was hurled from the line of scrimmage, Nagurski to Bill Hewitt. As Hewitt was about to be tackled, he tossed a long lateral pass to Karr. Karr caught it in the open and started for the goal line. Strong and another Giant defender tore after him, but Ronzani blocked out Strong, and Karr raced across with the winning points.

The Scoring:

Chicago	3	3	10	7	—	23
NY	0	7	7	7	—	21

Chi.—FG Manders 16
NY —Badgro 29, Newman pass (Strong kick)
Chi.—FG Manders 19
NY —Krause 1, run (Strong kick)
Chi.—Karr 8, Nagurski pass (Manders kick)
NY —Strong 8, Newman pass (Strong kick)
Chi.—Karr 32, lateral from Hewitt, Nagurski pass

The Statistics:

Touchdowns: (Bears) Karr (2).
(Giants) Badgro, Krause, Strong.

Field Goals: (Bears) Manders (3).

Points After Touchdown: (Bears) Brumbaugh, Manders.
(Giants) Strong (3).

X

WASHINGTON REDSKINS VS. CHICAGO BEARS
(Game played December 12, 1937)

CHICAGO, ILL. (Dec. 13, 1937)—When Sammy Baugh jogged off the field in the waning moments of the fourth quarter yesterday afternoon in Wrigley Field, 15,878 cold-numbed fans stood up and applauded with appreciative gusto.

It was a rare accolade.

It was a remarkable tribute for two reasons. Most of those 16,000 shivering spectators were rabid Chicago Bear boosters—and "Slingin' Sam" wore the uniform of the Washington Redskins. And the Redskins had won the ball game for the championship of the National Football League, 28-21.

But so great was Baugh's performance in this winner-take-all battle for prestige and money (a $225 for the winners as opposed to $127 for the losers) that this chilled and disappointed crowd could not help but acknowledge the magnitude of his accomplishments. He was the difference. He was greatness.

And he was the nonpareil as a first-year professional in this most grueling of professional leagues. Just the year before, he had been an All-American at Texas Christian University, and just this summer he had been captain of the College All Stars when they defeated the Green Bay Packers, 6-0, in Soldier Field. He has been great all the way—but perhaps never more so than in that "world" championship game of American-style football.

Playing conditions were wretched: 15-degree wind-scoured weather and a field encrusted with ice. It is amazing that nearly 16,000 hardy fans showed up for the game—and in fact, stayed through it—in cold so bitter that bonfires were lit here and there in the park as the game wore on.

But despite the weather and a bruising Bear line that rushed unmercifully—and, indeed, sent him to the locker room for treatment of a badly bruised leg late in the second quarter—Baugh was truly the difference. He was Washington's vital man, and he did everything he had to do. By the time the game was over he had completed 18 of 33 passes for 352 yards and had figured in all 4 of the Redskin TDs. And Baugh not only passed the ball; he handled it with expertise in every way to set up teammates' gains—besides his devastating punting and sound defensing.

Just the week before he had hit 11 for 15 in decidedly better weather to whip the New York Giants for yesterday's shot at the playoffs, capping a sensational freshman season. Sunday he won in icicle-cold weather. And so, even morose Bear fans paid him grudging respect.

Yet it took a magnificent third quarter for the Redskins to win. They struck 3 times (and Chicago once) during that lurid 15-minute span. It was a game with scores like 7-0 Washington, 7-7, 14-7 Chicago, 14-14, 21-14 Washington, 21-21, and finally 28-21 Washington. All in the exciting first 3 quarters. After which came a scoreless final quarter—but still exciting.

Baugh let the crowd (which had huddled under the stands right up to kickoff time in a vain effort to keep warm as long as possible) and his opposition know in a hurry just what Washington intended to do. On the first play, he unleashed a long pass to Cliff Battles for 43 yards to get the Redskins out of the hole after a deep opening kickoff. It was a typical tailback pass—the kind Baugh has become famous for—and audaciously thrown from his end zone. The pass gave Washington a vastly improved field position, but the Bears held. However, they too had to punt, and Washington took over on its own 47.

This time Washington scored. Twice Baugh missed on passes, but then came up with 3 straight strikes: first to Riley Smith, then to Ernie Pinckert, and then to Smith again to move the ball to the Chicago 16. From there he was content to simply pound the ball on the ground, and it was Battles who took it the last 7 on a scoot around right end. Smith then booted the extra point making it 7-0, and Washington had demonstrated its potent pass-rush versatility.

Chicago was by no means daunted, however. Taking over on its 28 after the kickoff, it threw a scare into the Skins in a hurry. On second down, Bernie Masterson dropped back and hit Jack Manders with an up-the-middle pass for 51 yards to the 11, only a great tackle by Battles preventing it from going all the way. It was only a temporary halt, for 2 plays later Manders ripped to the right on a quick-opener and was in the end zone. The big halfback then booted the extra point and it was 7-all.

Soon after, it was 14-7. Washington moved 29 yards in 5 plays after Manders' kickoff soared into the end zone, but an interception ended the brief march at midfield.

Once Chicago got the ball, it wasted no time scoring. Twice Manders banged for 9 yards, then Ray Nolting for 3, and it was first down on the Redskin 37. On the next play Manders was sent deep, and nabbed a pass from Masterson that went for a TD. Manders' placement then boosted it to 14.

That is how the score stood at half time, neither team having mustered another threat before the intermission. But Washington suffered a grave threat to its chances when Baugh had to be helped from the field with a painful leg injury. By the time the teams returned to the gridiron for the second half, however, the durable Texan was ready to go again. And how he did go!

It took just 5 plays to tie the score. Bull Irwin ran the kickoff back to the 32, then in 3 plays advanced the ball to the 45 for a first down. Then Wayne Millner, angling through the secondary, snatched a bullet pass from Baugh just past the midfield stripe. Manders couldn't catch him, and it was 14-all on Smith's place-kick.

Here the Bears showed their raw power. An annoyed Manders grabbed the kickoff and blasted over 2 men to return it from the 5 to his 28. Bronko Nagurski lunged for 6, and then Manders took the ball on a quick-opener and racked up 23 more, again busting over tacklers along the way. Two rushes by Nolting got another first down on the 35. And on the next play it was Nagurski again, the powerful Bear fullback this time running down tough Turk Edwards for 19 ploughing yards. When 3 more smashes by Manders and Nagurski made it first down on the 3, the Bears seemed unstoppable.

But those last 3 yards came hard. Nagurski was stymied going wide and lateraled to Masterson, who bobbled the ball and then hurled an incomplete pass. And when another pass failed, it was third down and still 3 to go. Washington massed an 8-man line to stop an anticipated run, but Masterson simply flipped over center to Eggs Manske for a TD. Manders added the PAT, and the Bears were out front again, 21-14.

Once again, however, Washington scored with sensational quickness. It got the ball on its 23 and sent Millner deep on the first play, picking up a fast 6 points when the rangy end nabbed Baugh's pass just over the 50 and outran Nagurski and Manders to the goal line. Smith's kick knotted things at 21-all.

Chicago got a march going after the kickoff but stalled at midfield and had to kick. Washington took over on its 20 when the boot soared into the end zone.

And again the Redskins took it all the way. Irwin started them off with 9 through the middle off a spread, then 7 more. One first down. Irwin got 2 yards. A pass missed, but in the critical third-down situation Baugh connected with Charley Malone for 10 and Washington had another first down. Next Baugh hit Millner for 8, then it was young Irwin belting the line twice for 2. Another first down. Baugh then pitched a quickie to Irwin for 7 to set up a difficult-to-defend situation—and Smith made the most of it. Smith called on Baugh to fake a pass to Malone (drawing the defense over), then drop back still more and fire to Charley Justice instead. "Choo-Choo" hauled it in on the run and galloped the last few strides into the end zone to complete a 35-yard scoring gain.

In all, during that sensational third-quarter outburst, Baugh completed 7 of 9 passes for 220 yards and 3 touchdowns. And all this while bothered by a bad leg.

When Smith kicked the extra point, it was 28-21, and Washington had all the points it needed for victory and the championship.

Still, though, Chicago was very much in the game, and twice in the remaining time it penetrated far enough into Washington territory to send additional shivers through the estimated 3,000 Redskin fans. On its first sally early in the final quarter, it advanced to the Washington 24 (a 32-yard aerial from Ray Buivid to Pug Rentner being the big gainer). But unaccountably, instead of sticking to its punishing ground game, it tried 4 straight passes—and all 4 went incomplete. Later in the period, Washington drove inside the Chicago 20 but fumbled, and Bill Conkright covered the ball to give the Bears possession on the 14. That not

Otto Graham (60), one
of the top passers in
football, picks up 12
yards by the overland
route in the first
quarter.

With mixed emotions, players on both teams watch closely as the kick by Lou Groza sails cleanly through the uprights with the winning 3 points. *(U.P.I.)*

Marion Motley (76) picks up 9 yards for the Browns in the third quarter.

"Automatic" Jack
Manders (far right)
kicks the first of his
3 field goals of the
afternoon, Carl
Brumbaugh holding
the ball. *(U.P.I.)*

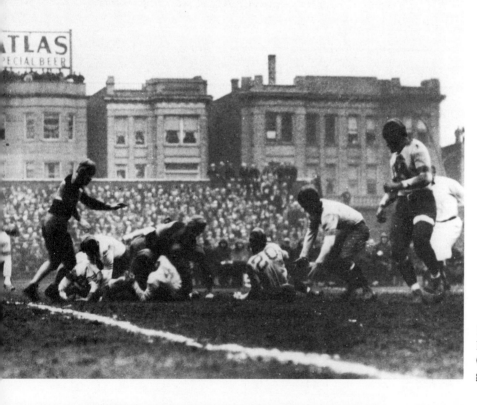

Red Grange picks up a
lost lateral pass from
Carl Brumbaugh (8) and
goes for 3 yards. *(U.P.I.)*

GAME 10
Washington Redskins vs.
Chicago Bears
December 12, 1937

Chicago's Dick Plasman takes a 35-yard pass from Keith Molesworth in the final quarter. He was finally knocked out of bounds by Sammy Baugh. *(U.P.I.)*

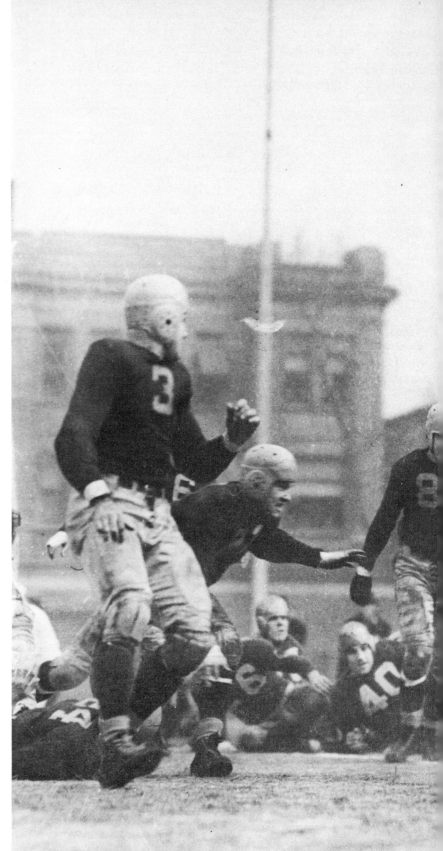

Cliff Battles (20) is stopped by Joe Stydahar of the Bears for no gain late in the third quarter. Sammy Baugh (3) looks on. *(U.P.I.)*

GAME 11
Cleveland Rams vs.
Washington Redskins
December 16, 1945

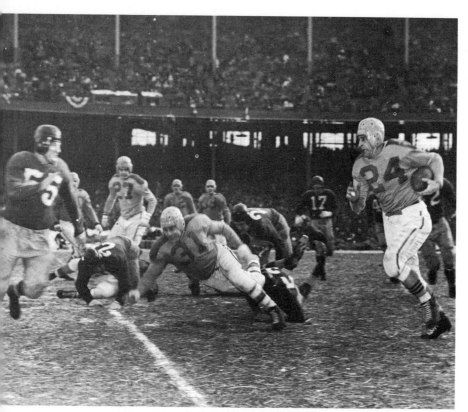

Cleveland Rams'
fullback, Jim Gillette
(24), sweeps around his
left end for a 4-yard
gain in the third quarter
as Redskin center, Ky
Aldrich (55), moves in
for the tackle. *(U.P.I.)*

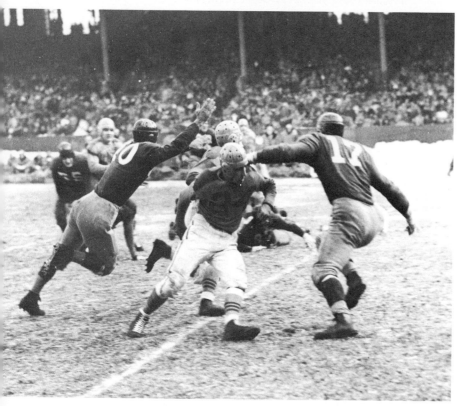

Redskin end Wayne
Millner (40) and tackle
Fred Davis (17)
surround Ram Jim
Gillette (24) even
though he doesn't have
the ball. The ball is
being carried by Don
Greenwood, behind
Gillette. *(U.P.I.)*

only saved an impending Redskin score, but also started the Bears off on one last threatening march that was to gain 79 yards in 5 plays.

One of those plays was a 35-yard pass from Keith Molesworth to Dick Plasman that wound up with Baugh jolting him out of bounds in front of the Redskin bench. Just who started the fight depends on whose testimony is believed, but a fight certainly erupted between the teams.

Having swept to the Washington 7-yard line in a relentless fashion, the Bears seemed certain to take it all the way—but on third down and short yardage, Masterson slipped trying to evade the charging rush of huge Turk Edwards and was thrown for a 7-yard loss. And when a fourth-down pass into the end zone failed, the last real Bruin threat was over.

During the scoreless final quarter the Redskins recovered a fumble, blocked a punt in their own territory, and intercepted one last pass just before the gun.

It had been essentially a Baugh triumph (as all-time pro great Earl "Dutch" Clark of Detroit said, "He is the greatest passer I've ever seen"), and the statistics show it. He completed 18 of 33 passes for 3 touchdowns, gaining 335 yards—and as an auxiliary weapon carried the ball himself 3 times for gains of 3, 12, and 17. However, a huge 26-yard first-quarter loss when trapped trying to pass left him with a net 6-yard gain on the ground.

In his amazing rookie season, Baugh completed 99 of 304 passes for 1,463 yards in a dozen games—and had only 15 interceptions.

Those remarkable statistics are testimony to the endless hours Baugh spent in developing his passing skills as a teen-ager. Too scrawny to have much of an opportunity to make his high school team, he was determined to become so expert at throwing a football that he would have to be given a chance to play despite his size. So day after day, for long hour after hour, he would practice spiraling a football through an automobile tire. He threw at a motionless tire at first, then swinging back and forth; he threw at it standing still and running and changing direction in every conceivable way. Eventually he became uncannily accurate. And he not only got his chance to play but became a Texas high school sensation. Perseverance did it.

Yet, despite his prowess at throwing a football, it was his baseball credentials that earned him a scholarship to Texas Christian. By his junior year—having now mastered the art of punting just as he had passing—he was the Horned Frogs' bellwether. Earning the nickname "Slingin' Sam," he wound up guiding TCU to a Sugar Bowl triumph and himself to All-American honors.

Still, though, Baugh felt that baseball would be his best bet for a professional career. Lean and lanky, he felt that in baseball he could last—whereas in rugged pro football, injury could cut his playing years short at any time. And he was a skilled shortstop. So Baugh signed with the St. Louis farm system, only to discover belatedly that another young shortstop by the name of Marty "Slats" Marion was there ahead of him—and destined for certain stardom. Still, he stuck it out in baseball through the season, demonstrating that he was a fine infielder, but as long as Marion was around, he faced a long minor league career in the vast Cardinal chain.

As it happened, George Preston Marshall had decided to abandon Boston and move his franchise elsewhere at this time. Last year he had a Redskin team that was good enough to win the Eastern division title but simply did not attract crowds. So for the championship playoff game with the Green Bay Packers, Marshall decided to switch the contest from Boston to New York. It drew nearly 30,000 largely neutral fans and convinced him it would be folly to return to Boston. Washington became his choice.

Even though the Redskins lost that 1936 playoff to the Packers, 21-6 (Battles went out with a leg injury shortly after it began), Marshall and Coach Ray Flaherty had assembled a first-rate football team. It was studded with talent such as Cliff Battles, Pug Rentner, Ernie Pinckert, Riley Smith, Wayne Millner, Turk Edwards, and others of championship caliber. Only a passer was lacking. Marshall got that passer in Baugh. He convinced Samuel Adrian Baugh that he should give pro football a try, and in June the lanky 6-2 Texan signed.

How much he signed for nobody has been able to find out, and the guesses have ranged from $7,000 all the way up to $20,000 and more. All the Redskins say is that he is the highest paid professional football player ever.

Whatever the sum, Sammy fully earned it on Sunday.

The Scoring:

Washington	7	0	21	0	—	28
Chicago	14	0	7	0	—	21

Wash.—Battles 7, run (Smith kick)
Chi.—Manders 10, run (Manders kick)
Wash.—Manders 37, Masterson pass (Manders kick)
Wash.—Millner 55, Baugh pass (Smith kick)
Chi.—Manske 3, Masterson pass (Manders kick)
Wash.—Millner 78, Baugh pass (Smith kick)
Wash.—Justice 35, Baugh pass (Smith kick)

The Statistics:

	Chi.	Wash.
First downs	11	18
Rushing yardage	128	70
Passing yardage	207	371
Passes	8-31	22-40
Own passes intercepted	3	3
Fumbles lost	0	2
Penalties	1-15	1-5

XI

CLEVELAND RAMS VS. WASHINGTON REDSKINS
(Game played December 16, 1945)

CLEVELAND, OHIO (Dec. 17, 1945)—Goalposts decided the National Football League championship here yesterday.

Cleveland's Rams eked out a bizarre 15-14 victory over the Washington Redskins in near-zero temperature on the snow-piled field of Municipal Stadium. It was a miserable Sunday for football, both for the two teams and for the 32,178 cold-tormented spectators.

But the teams and fans suffered through a closely fought ball game that was unique in the annals of NFL playoffs—and eminently worth the risk of frostbite. Victory could have gone to either team, but it went to Cleveland because of 3 points directly attributable to the goalposts. That's right—the goalposts! Twice balls struck the wooden structures—and both times the occurrence benefited the Rams.

The first time it happened was midway through the opening quarter when the Redskins' Sammy Baugh attempted a pass from the end zone and the ball hit one of the uprights and rebounded into the end zone for an automatic safety: 2 points for Cleveland. Just the play before, after making a tremendous goal-line stand, Washington had been penalized to its 2½-yard line when Baugh intentionally grounded a pass.

The second time was late in the second quarter on an extra-point place-kick by Bob Waterfield. A charging Redskin partially blocked the kick, but the ball carried just far and high enough to strike the crossbar, totter for a moment, and then dropped over: 1 more point for Cleveland. In such a way was the 1945 championship decided.

There was, needless to say, much, much more to the game than those 2 freak happenings. It was a first-rate contest worthy of playoff stature.

Unfortunately, Washington was plagued not only by the 2 goalpost episodes but also by injuries—and most especially besetting its premier passer, Baugh. The great Texan was bothered by a floating rib, although he insisted that he was well enough to play. But he threw only 6 passes and completed only 1—and that for just 5 yards. Frank Filchock, however, did a fine job of filling in for Baugh and hit on 8 of 14 for 174 yards.

Moreover, husky Frank Akins, the second-best ground gainer in the league, suffered a broken nose on the first play of the game and had to retire permanently to the bench after running 2 more plays, further crippling the Washington attack.

But the chief reason for the Redskin defeat, even more than Baugh's injury and the weird goalpost doings, was the complete breakdown of their rushing attack. The ordinarily formidable Skins could produce only 32 yards on the ground. The only poorer running yardage total in a playoff game was 22 by the 1940 Redskins against the Chicago Bears.

Cleveland's aerial game produced the unquestioned game standouts. Bob Waterfield was everything he had been touted to be, connecting on 14 of 27 passes for 172 yards and 2 TDs, while finessing the ball nicely at the "T." And in halfback Jim Gillette and end Jim Benton (the leading pass receiver of the league) he had extraordinary catchers, even on this nippy day. Gillette lugged the ball for 101 additional yards in 17 carries to illustrate his versatility.

Rams' Coach Adam Walsh maintained that "if the field had been good, we'd have beaten the tar out of 'em," noting that several times Waterfield's adroit ball handling fooled the Redskins and shot men into the clear, but they were unable to go all the way on the icy footing.

Cleveland made the first serious threat of the game, marching 74 yards before finally being halted on the Washington 5-yard line. Then came the penalty on grounding a pass and the subsequent fluke safety against Baugh and 2 points. Nine and a half minutes remained in the first quarter.

Not until 15 more minutes had gone by did another score go on the board. Ky Aldrich intercepted a Waterfield pass to give the Redskins possession on their 48. Shortly after, a roughing penalty was called, and the ball was further advanced to the Ram 38.

Two plays later, Washington scored. After Steve Bagarus was

held on a run, he was sent out for a pass on the next play and took Filchock's toss all the way. He eluded a skidding Waterfield and then sprinted the last dozen yards to the goal line unmolested. When Joe Aguirre booted the extra point, it was a 7-2 ball game after 5 and a half minutes of the second period.

But the lead did not last long. Cleveland slammed back 80 yards, led by Gillette's wide swings and Waterfield's throws. The attack seemed in danger of being halted when the latter was tossed for a 5-yard loss back to his own 48. But he responded with a 15-yard pitch to Benton, and the Rams were down on the 37. Another toss to Benton and the Rams were "home," the nifty end streaking past the secondary into the clear on the 12 and racing the rest of the way with Redskins in futile chase. Then came Waterfield's successful PAT for 9-7 as the ball survived partial blocking and its momentary contact with the crossbar.

Before the half ended, Cleveland threatened briefly as Pat West intercepted a pass, enabling the Rams to get to the Washington 12, only to have Aldrich, in turn, intercept to avert the danger.

It didn't take long for the Rams to increase their meager 2-point advantage once the second half began. They went 81 yards with the kickoff to boost things to 15-7. The payoff strike came right after a penalty for man-in-motion that set the Rams back 5 yards to the Washington 44. This time it was Gillette who got the call to head upfield for a pass. He pulled in the ball on the 14, gave his man the slip, and continued on for the score. Waterfield missed the placement following the TD.

Down by 8 points and therefore needing more than a TD and PAT to win, the Redskins obviously had to move—but for most of the remainder of the third quarter it was Cleveland that controlled the ball, and generally in Washington territory. With only a few minutes remaining in the quarter, the Skins finally did something.

The attack began on the Washington 30. First Bob Defruiter picked up a big 15 yards, then Filchock lobbed a long pass upfield to Bagarus that took the Redskins all the way to the 6 before Fred Gehrke tackled him. When Gil Booley speared through the line to hurl Filchock back to the 17, Washington's attacking plan obviously had to be altered. Twice it sent backs into the line—Merlyn Condit for 3, Sal Rossaro for 6. Now the ball was on the 8-yard line and third down with goal to go.

Filchock went back to pass and somehow kept eluding the charge of onrushing Rams sufficiently long to find an open receiver, Bob Seymour, who had just come into the game for Bagarus. Seymour got free "all by his lonesome" for an easy catch and a score. It had been a superb bit of evasive action by Filchock. When Aguirre booted the extra point, the gap was closed to a single point at 15-14. Eight seconds remained in the third period.

The remaining 15 minutes of the final quarter produced only zeroes for both teams. Twice Washington got within field-goal range but was unable to put the ball between the uprights—once when Aguirre was wide from the 31, again when he was short from the 46.

And time kept working against the Redskins. It finally came down to one more chance when Waterfield—who had punted magnificently all game long (twice kicked out of bounds inside the 10) put one more punt out of bounds at the Washington 15 with only half a minute remaining. Filchock could do only one thing: pass. And an alert Albie Reisz intercepted on the 30 to squelch that last chance. Thereafter Waterfield just flopped on the ball as time ran out.

Thus ended a game played in weather so cold that even the instruments of the colorful Redskin band froze and made music impossible at the half-time interlude. For Cleveland it was a fitting end to a fine season in which it reeled off a 9-1 record in capturing the Western division with ease—as against Washington's hard struggle to beat out Philadelphia by a single game, compiling an 8-2 Eastern record. And it was the first Cleveland title since the playoff system had begun in 1933, its second since 1924 in NFL competition.

But Washington Coach Dud DeGroot couldn't help but feel that had Baugh been in tip-top shape, his Redskins could have taken it all. Since Baugh had joined the club in 1937, Washington had won divisional laurels in 1937, 1940, 1942, 1943, and 1945 and "the works" in 1937 and 1942. The lean Texan had completed an amazing 70.3 percent of his passes for his best season ever. And not only was he sorely missed on attack, he was a grave loss defensively. An early-season game against the New York Giants tellingly illustrated this—besides throwing 2 touchdown passes, he knocked down 2 end-zone passes, ran 71 yards with an interception, and made at least 7 tackles from his safety position. Without question, the 6-foot-2 star—who had preferred baseball as a career just could not be replaced in the Washington lineup.

Nevertheless, on overall balance, Cleveland has demonstrated that it is a truly great football team and one that could remain so for some years to come.

The Scoring:

Washington	0	7	7	0	—	14
Cleveland	2	7	6	0	—	15

Clev.—safety, Baugh pass hits goalpost
Wash.—Bagarus 38, Filchock pass (Aguirre kick)
Clev.—Benton 37, Waterfield pass (Waterfield kick)
Wash.—Gillette 56, Waterfield pass (Waterfield kick failed)
Clev.—Seymour 8, Filchock pass (Aguirre kick)

The Statistics:

	Clev.	Wash.
First downs	14	8
Rushing yardage	180	35
Passing yardage	192	179
Passes	14-27	9-20
Own passes intercepted	2	2
Punting	8-38	7-36
Fumbles lost	1	0
Penalties	6-60	4-34

XII

DETROIT LIONS VS. CLEVELAND BROWNS
(Game played December 27, 1953)

DETROIT, MICH. (Dec. 28, 1953)—Bobby Layne the magnificent, using all the guile and skill he has in abundance, rallied the Detroit Lions to a stirring 17-16 victory over the Cleveland Browns here yesterday afternoon in a flamboyant last-minute finish.

Layne led the Lions 80 yards in the final drive, throwing a touchdown strike to Jim Doran with just 2 minutes and 8 seconds left in the game. It was typical swashbuckling Layne.

Thus Detroit retains its championship of the National Football League—and continued its singular mastery over the formidable Browns. Do the Lions have a jinx on the Browns? Not once has Cleveland beaten Detroit since joining the NFL in 1950—and this with championship teams.

Until the Layne-led payoff drive, Cleveland appeared to at last have a victory before the 54,577 spectators in Briggs Stadium (not to mention the millions following the game on radio and TV). With just 4:10 left to play, Lou Groza booted a field goal that boosted the score to 16-10 and put Detroit out of field-goal range—and this in a game that had failed to produce any real offensive punch. Any Detroit retaliatory strike seemed remote.

But with time running out, Layne—that superlative master in the clutch—drove his Lions 80 yards to victory on a succession of passes and his own runs. And then, when Cleveland again got the ball after the kickoff, a pass interception by Carl Karilovacz nailed it down.

It was the third straight NFL championship playoff loss for the Browns following their stunning debut triumph in 1950 after being accepted into the league with the demise of the All-American Football Conference.

For the Lions it meant $2,424.10 each; for the Browns, $1,654.26.

This was basically a defensive brawl. Cleveland got 3 field goals and a single TD; Detroit 2 TDs and 1 field goal. The difference actually was Doak Walker's place-kick for a PAT after that final touchdown. In fact, Walker had 11 points via his own touchdown, a field goal, and 2 extra points. Layne hit on 12 of 25 passes, picking up 179 net yards—and rushed for 44 more. Cleveland's Otto Graham had one of his rare bad days: He frequently missed passes (both too long and too short) and completed a nearly unbelievable 2 of 15 for 31 yards. When "yards thrown trying to pass" are taken into account, it amounts to a net of 9 yards gained overhead. (George Ratterman completed 1 pass and also lost ground trying another.) And Graham was the league's leading passer . . . until yesterday!

Detroit scored first in just over 4 minutes. Burly Joe Schmidt creamed Graham on Cleveland's second play from scrimmage after the opening kickoff, forcing a fumble—and huge (300 pounds-plus) Les Bingaman recovered on the Brown 13.

Four plays later Detroit was on the 3 with a hard-earned first down, the Browns hanging tough all the way. Bob Hoernschemeyer belted to the 1, and then Walker took it over left guard into the end zone. And when Walker added the extra point, it was 7-0.

That was the only scoring in the opening period, however. Cleveland had Detroit cooped up inside their 5-yard line later on and threw Layne back to the 1—only to be penalized 15 yards for roughness, which gave the Lion QB room to operate.

Later in the quarter, Len Ford recovered a Hoernschemeyer fumble on the Lion 6-yard line to provide a great scoring chance—but Cleveland couldn't push it over. Groza then booted a 14-yard field goal to make it 7-3 seconds after the second period began; it was his twenty-fourth of the season.

By half time, however, Detroit had boosted its lead to 10-3 on a Walker field goal. He was short on one try from the 45, but made good on another from the 22.

The kick followed a "tricky" play on which officials first were fooled but then concurred that a Detroit TD was not allowable. Jim David had intercepted a pass on the Cleveland 20. Layne took the snap on the first play, pitched to Walker, and raced off into the secondary to take a pass from Doak for a touchdown. But

Cleveland objected, pointing out that Layne was less than a yard from center and therefore ineligible as a receiver. The play was recalled, and Detroit was penalized 15 yards.

So what did Layne do? He passed the Lions back to the 20 enabling Walker to kick his field goal. Detroit got an extra 5 yards when Cleveland was offside, enabling the FG try to be made from the 23.

As the half ended, Groza tried a 51-yarder but it sailed wide—his only miss.

Coming back in the second half, Cleveland looked much sharper than it had in the first 30 minutes. In less than 7 minutes, it scored. Actually, it swept 51 yards for a touchdown in just 8 plays—7 of which were on the ground. The chief ball-toters were Billy Reynolds and Ray Renfro, along with a couple of carries by Graham. Immediately Harry Jagade zipped off right tackle for the score. Groza kicked the point, and it was 10-all midway through the period.

Cleveland went out front as the final quarter began. It moved 49 yards on a drive as the third period ended, to position itself on the Detroit 7-yard line with second down. Renfro missed a Graham pass, and the Browns' QB took it himself for a short gain to set Groza up for another field-goal attempt. With 16 seconds having elapsed in the last period, Groza banged it home: 13-10.

And before too long it was 16-10. Detroit got close enough for Walker to attempt a field goal from 33 yards out, but it went wide. And then Cleveland moved. A sparkling 30-yard run by Jagade was the prime mover, but after 3 more plays the attack stalled on the 35. So once more Groza got the call, and the big man punched it home from the 43: 16-10. And 4:10 left to play.

Groza compounded problems for Detroit by kicking the kickoff over the goal line, making the Lions take over on the 20 without a chance for a runback. But Layne now became the dominant figure in the ball game. Slippery though the ground was, the Lions went all the way. All but 2 of those 80 yards were gained on Layne passes to Doran (3 catches) and Cloyce Box (1). Layne himself lugged the ball twice. Detroit swept upfield crisply to a first down on the Cleveland 34. Layne sent Doran toward the end zone. Doran beat his man and pulled it in for the score.

Doran was subbing for Leon Hart, the great Lion end who had been hurt in the first quarter and was sitting out the rest of the game. It was Doran's first touchdown of the season—and one that must have given him intense satisfaction. Before the season began, after Coach Buddy Parker had gone to bat for him in a prolonged pay hassle with management, he had promised during the discussions "I'll win the championship for you, coach"—and so he did on Sunday.

The Lions' bench could claim partial credit for the winning pass. It was they who noted that the Cleveland secondary was playing up close to the Detroit ends. "So I faked a block going out and then cut around a defense man," said Doran, "and when I reached the end zone and look up, there was the ball."

Still, though, there was time for Cleveland to come back. But when Karilovacz intercepted Graham's pass shortly after the kickoff, it was all over. Detroit had only to run out the clock, and it did.

It was a gloomy ending for the Browns, Paul Brown morosely commented, "It was the toughest game we've ever lost." In fact, added the veteran coach, "I doubt if any team ever lost a tougher one."

The game also ended a season that for most of the fall and winter seemed destined to be one of the truly great ones of pro football. The Browns went into their final league game possessors of a gaudy 11-0 record, that eleventh triumph having been achieved via a spectacular 62-14 win over their bitter rivals, the New York Giants. Relief quarterback George Ratterman hurled 3 TD passes and helped the team to more than 500 yards total offense. That left only one more game for a perfect season, but Philadelphia took care of any such notions with a smashing 42-27 upset.

So the goal of an unbeaten season was dashed in the final game of the regular schedule—and now the championship quest as well. To many Cleveland partisans, the season was almost too easy; by November 15, when the Browns edged San Francisco, 23-21, the divisional crown had been in the bag, and sustaining momentum undoubtedly became increasingly difficult in the ensuing weeks. Certainly the Browns appeared lackluster against the Eagles, and although they roused themselves for yesterday's championship playoff, they just could not pull off a win in the style they had shown early in the campaign.

Analyzing the regular season by halves, one can see why: The offense generated somewhat more points in the second half—193 to 155; and the defense gave up vastly more in its last 6 games, yielding 125 as against a meager 37 in the first six outings. Certainly they lost momentum.

Detroit, on the other hand, started out in lackluster fashion but came on strong. It lost 2 of its first 6 starts, then reeled off 6 straight. It was a going ball club.

It also was a ball club with Bobby Layne. And although Otto Graham may have been the league's leading passer, Layne has both the immense technical qualifications and charisma that so often combine to win the big ones. And Sunday was a big one.

Layne "informed" Coach Buddy Parker early in the 1952 season, after the Lions had lost 2 of their first 3 games despite being touted as a title contender, that he was going to be the quarterback. Thereafter the Lions lost only once that year, and that by a point to the Chicago Bears. And he also led them to a 17-7 conquest of Cleveland in last year's championship playoff. All of which led to this year's 10-2 record and another crack at the Browns—and again a winning one.

Layne, face it, is a catalyst. He is a Texan, much like Sammy Baugh in the '40s. Baugh was perhaps the most accurate passer, the supreme technician, a great all-around football player (including being one of the finest punters ever)—and also a superlative clutch-man. Layne is Layne: also a pro who undoubtedly would have been great defensively had he played in the days before platooning—and utterly the nonpareil for delivering in the pinch. He had what they call *machismo* south of the border. He had style. He epitomized the Texas Legend.

Born in 1926 in the small town of Santa Ana, Lyne was adopted by relatives at the age of 6 and moved to Fort Worth. Before long he had moved (with the people he always called "Mom and Dad," the Wade Hamptons) to Dallas—and it was there he went to high school. He started out as a guard but quickly became a tailback in the single-wing offense of the era.

111

A youth called Doak Walker was a freshman when Layne was a sophomore, and the two became close friends—and top ball players on the Highland Park High School team. Both were keen competitors, and both helped each other work at improving their skills long after regular practice ceased. Highland gained statewide recognition because of them.

But Layne wasn't just a footballer. In 1943 he was the ace pitcher of the community's American Legion team and helped it win the state championship. As Baugh had done a decade before, he wound up with a baseball scholarship at a Texas university—although his was Texas U. On a team that boasted Randy Jackson (later to be a major leaguer), he won an amazing 26 games in conference play—without a loss—and participated in the national tournament in his senior year, although the Longhorns did not win the title.

He also played football at Texas U. under Dana X. Bible, running the old single-wing. Then he took time off for a stint in the Merchant Marine (along with Walker—who then transferred to Southern Methodist). In his senior year, Blair Cherry took over for Bible and switched from the traditional offense to the new T-formation. For Layne, a natural tailback, it was a difficult transition (as it was for Baugh at the same time in the pro game), but he did it. He and his bride traveled to the Chicago Cardinals' training camp for a forum on the new technique, along with Cherry, and he adapted quickly. In fact, in that senior year Texas lost but a single game—and that by a point to SMU and Walker (Texas had won the other 2 tilts in Layne's rivalry with his former prep teammate).

By 1948 the All-American Football Conference was trying hard to enlist players in bucking the NFL, but Layne stuck with the established circuit. Pittsburgh had selected him as its No. 1 draft choice, but Bobby let the Steelers know that he was more interested in a T-quarterback team than one that ran the old single-wing. Nevertheless, Pittsburgh picked him up, then traded him to the Bears, where he was a distant third string behind two greats, Sid Luckman and Johnny Lujack. In 1949 he was traded to the dismal (1-17-1) New York Bulldogs. He was again traded after the season, this time to the Lions. Because of coach

Bo McMillan's yen for calling plays from the bench, he was decidedly unhappy. Eventually a player protest resulted in Buddy Parker's replacing Bo as coach.

By last year the Lions had developed into world champions, with Layne leading the pride. On Sunday they did it again—and again with Layne at the head. He is that kind of man.

The Scoring:

Detroit	7	3	0	7	—	17
Cleveland	0	3	7	6	—	16

Det.—Walker 1, run (Walker kick)
Clev.—FG Groza 13
Det.—FB Walker 23
Clev.—Jagade 9, run (Groza kick)
Clev.—FG Groza 15
Clev.—FG Groza 43
Det.—Doran 33, Layne pass (Walker kick)

The Statistics:

	Det.	Clev.
First downs	18	11
Rushing yardage	129	182
Passing yardage	179	9
Passes	12-25	3-16
Own passes intercepted	2	2
Punting	4-49	5-42
Fumbles lost	2	2
Penalties	50	30

XIII

PHILADELPHIA EAGLES VS. GREEN BAY PACKERS
(Game played December 26, 1960)

PHILADELPHIA, PA. (Dec. 27, 1960)—The Eagles came up with the big plays—both on attack and defense yesterday, so now Philadelphia rules as National Football League champion. They defeated a stubborn Green Bay Packer team, 17-13, Monday afternoon on the thawing bog-like turf of Franklin Field. The Packers had the yards, but the Eagles had the points—that's what it came down to.

It also came down to one of the most dramatic last plays in the many years of NFL playoff games. Playoffs have been won—and lost—with seconds to go, but except for "sudden death" there has always been a play or two left in which to challenge the outcome. And rarely have those last plays been anything but despairing gestures. Yesterday the game ended literally on a final play that pitted a tremendous young runner against an ultimately unflinching veteran in a magnificent *mano a mano* conclusion. Those who were there will never forget that confrontation.

The Packers had made a gallant last-minute drive down to the Philadelphia 22 with seconds left—so few seconds that the next play would obviously be the last one. For that last play, quarterback Bart Starr went to the Packer whose unquenchably fierce drive is the greatest of all on this fighting team: Jim Taylor, his fullback. He could have gambled on a long pass into the end zone, but the Eagles were in a "prevent" umbrella defense against deep passes, and if that one long throw failed, it would be all over. So Starr went to the short pass that was certain to be caught, betting on Taylor's magnificent desire to ram it home.

It almost worked. Taylor caught the toss at the line of scrimmage and burst upfield. He fought his way through the first of the Eagle defenders and twisted and lurched as far as his churning legs would take him before one of the all-time greats of professional football, Chuck Bednarik (the captain of the Eagles' defensive unit) slammed into him and literally fought him down in a clash of muscle. The ball was on the 9-yard line.

That is where the game ended and how it ended. Green Bay had a first down, but no more time.

The 67,325 fans watching the game in sunny 43-degree weather saw a contest in which the Wisconsin team dominated play but was thwarted by a stout Philadelphia defense when it counted. Green Bay ran off 77 plays and gained 401 yards, Philadelphia 48 plays for 296 yards. Moreover, besides its decided offensive advantage, the Packer defense pounced on 2 fumbles and intercepted 2 passes—as against a solitary fumble recovery for the Eagles and no interceptions.

On the basis of the attacking statistics and the defensive turnovers, one would reasonably expect that this was a Green Bay triumph. Indeed, 7 times the Packers had chances to score in Eagle territory, but came away with a paltry 2 field goals and 1 touchdown. Consider the penetrations:

> First quarter—to the Eagle 14- and 23-yard lines.
> Second quarter—to the Eagle 17 and 7.
> Third quarter—to the Eagle 26.
> Fourth quarter—to the Eagle 8 and 9.

Nevertheless, for all the chances Green Bay had, it was Philadelphia that most frequently came up with the big play— more aptly, perhaps, the right play at the right time—to earn victory in this collision between divisional champions of East and West.

It was Philadelphia's rugged defenses headed by Bednarik (lauded by Packer offensive end Gary Knafelc after the game as "one of the real pros; he's one of the toughest men I've ever met"). And it was an opportunist Philadelphia attack led by Norm Van Brocklin. (Said Packer Coach Vince Lombardi afterward, "Give Van all the credit in the world—he completed the big ones today!") More bluntly put was Packer defensive end Bill Quinlan's grudging accolade: "it was that damn Dutchman!"

The Dutchman did indeed have a fine day. It was by no means one of his great ones, but in his retiring performance (in fact, Van

116

Brocklin, Bednarik, and Coach Buck Shaw all had announced that they would be retiring immediately after the game—and in the Eagles' dressing room held to those statements), he did the job that a successful quarterback had to do: He put winning points on the scoreboard. Van Brocklin hit on 9 of 20 passes for 204 yards with 1 interception (the Packers also picked off one of his lateral "swing passes") and came up with some clutch heaves. One went for 35 yards to Tommy McDonald and a touchdown midway in the second quarter. Two others to Pete Retzlaff (for 41) and Ted Dean (for 22) later in the quarter set up Bobby Walston's field goal from the 15. And a pop-pass to Billy Barnes for a short but oh-so-vital 13 yards late in the final quarter was mightily helpful in setting up the winning ground touchdown.

The Dutchman did indeed have a fine day.

His counterpart, Bart Starr, had what Lombardi characterized as "not a great day—or a bad day. His only bad pass was when he missed Max McGee in the end zone early in the first quarter." His last-minute assault, though, was brilliant. Over the game, the former Alabama star threw 34 times and completed 21 for 178 yards but got only 1 TD. That one score was a 7-yard strike to McGee early in the fourth quarter. In the final minute and a half he directed the Packers with precision from their 35 to the Eagle 9 in 7 briskly executed plays.

Time was a critical factor for the Packers at the end of both the first half and the game. So too were inches. As to the latter, Taylor missed a first down by inches deep in Philly territory in both halves. Either time Green Bay could have gone for a short field goal, but both times it disdained the three-pointer for a shot at the big six. As to the time aspect, the Packers had a first down on the Eagle 7-yard line as time was running out in the first half and had to try a field goal from a difficult angle which missed; and they were on the 9-yard line with a meaningless first down as the game ended. Packer rooters and players could not help but agree with Lombardi's comment after the game that "if we'd had a few more seconds at the end of each half we'd have been all right."

But still, it is the team that makes the big play that so often wins, albeit outplayed—and Philadelphia most surely had those decisive plays. It had them right from the start.

117

The Eagles won the toss and elected to receive. Paul Hornung kicked off to Tim Brown on the 2, who brought it back to the 22. So what happened on the first play? It didn't go on the official "books" as a pass interception, but that's what it amounted to: A snatch by defensive end Quinlan of a lateral pitchout/pass by Van Brocklin gave Green Bay possession on Philadelphia's 14-yard line. It was a tremendous break for the Packers. Taylor then slammed for 5 on first down, putting the ball on the Eagle 9.

Then Philadelphia got tough. Hornung got 2 going to the left side, then Taylor swung inside left end for another yard to the 6: fourth and 2. Once more Taylor shot into the line, but the Eagles held him for a single yard gain—and by a measurement of inches they took over the ball inside their own 5. The Eagles had grudgingly yielded little ground.

Three plays later it started all over again. With the ball on the 10, Dean slanted off tackle but fumbled—and Bill Forester fell on the ball on the Philadelphia 22. Another break for the Packers.

Just like the previous time, Green Bay got a big 5 on its first down—this time by Hornung off right tackle. On the next play Taylor blew through the middle for 6, making it first down on the 11.

Again the Eagles toughened. Hornung went to the right for 3, but on the next play Taylor's 3 was off side, and the ball was moved back to the 13. And now Green Bay couldn't stay on the ground. So Starr passed into the end zone to Knafelc, but it went incomplete. Now the Packers *had* to pass, but this one to Max McGee also failed—the throw that Lombardi later felt was Starr's only bad throw of the day. Having been thwarted of any score the last time, Green Bay now went for the "sure" 3 points—and got them on Hornung's FG from the 20. With 6:20 elapsed, it was 3-0.

The Packers almost had an incredible third chance on the first play after the kickoff when Van Brocklin fumbled. But he recovered it himself, and Philadelphia had possession on its 22. Had he not covered it, it could have been disastrous.

The rest of the first quarter was so-so until the Packers took over on their 37 after a punt with only a couple of minutes left. Hornung and Taylor then belted for 9, and Starr adroitly passed to Knafelc for 8 to the Eagle 42 on a "fooler" third-and-1 situation.

118

GAME 12
Detroit Lions vs.
Cleveland Browns
December 27, 1953

Lion end Jim Doran
(83) catches a pass
from quarterback
Bobby Layne in the
final quarter.
Linebacker Warren
Lahr makes the tackle.
This set up the winning
touchdown, Layne to
Doran on the following
play. *(U.P.I.)*

Lions' Doak Walker (37) kicks the important point after Detroit's tying touchdown to give the Lions a 17-16 win. *(U.P.I.)*

GAME 13
Philadelphia Eagles vs.
Green Bay Packers
December 26, 1960

Chuck Bednarik, captain of the Eagles, tackles Paul Hornung behind the line of scrimmage in the first period. *(U.P.I.)*

Eagle defender Bobby Freeman (84) breaks up a pass intended for Green Bay's Gary Knafelc. *(U.P.I.)*

Norm Van Brocklin
(11) passes down field
to Tommy McDonald.
(U.P.I.)

Dallas Texans' Len
Dawson (16), guarded
by tackle Jerry
Cornelison (74),
evades Houston Oilers'
tackle Ed Husman (82)
and picks up 8 yards in
the second quarter.
(U.P.I.)

Oilers' halfback Billy
Cannon (20) looks for
a receiver downfield as
Texans' end Bill Hull
(85) moves in. Charlie
Hennigan (87) was
unable to stave off the
charge and Cannon was
downed after gaining 4
yards. *(U.P.I.)*

Oilers' halfback Billy
Cannon is bowled over
by the onrushing tide
of Texans as he picked
up 4 yards around right
end. Taking him down
are Jerry Mays (75),
Duane Wood (48), and
E. J. Holub (55).
(U.P.I.)

Taylor then ripped up the middle for 13 as the quarter ended. Two plays after the second quarter began, Starr flipped to Boyd Dowler for 15 down to the 14. Another big threat loomed.

But it died quickly. Taylor got 3 on first down, but the Packers were off side on the next play—an incomplete pass. Two more passes missed. But the Packers didn't come away with nothing, for Hornung booted another field goal, from the 23, making it 6-0 Packers. And Philadelphia had yet to do anything with its offense.

Philadelphia soon did something, however. It had to punt after one first down, the Packers taking over on their 20—but shortly they had to punt also. Philly took over on its 43. From there, it struck quickly. On first down Van Brocklin passed to Tommy McDonald for 22 yards to the Packer 35. Again Van Brocklin passed to McDonald, and this time it went all the way. When Walston kicked the extra point, all the Packer dominance to that point was obliterated, and it was a 7-6 ball game on 2 quick plays.

Of the McDonald strikes, both coaches had something to say. Shaw said in the dressing room after the game that he was "surprised McDonald was single-covered most of the afternoon, inasmuch as most teams in the Eastern Division put two men on him." Lombardi pointed out that "[defensive back] Hank Gremminger slipped on the ice—but that was just one of those things."

So Green Bay was behind, its early momentum eclipsed. And now the tide turned. When Philadelphia next got the ball on a punt on its 26, it moved upfield quickly—mostly on a 41-yard pass to Retzlaff and a 22-yarder to Dean—to the 8. But 3 Dutchman passes failed, and Philadelphia settled for a 15-yard field goal by Walston for 10-6.

Green Bay surged back, however. It took the kickoff on its 20 after Dean booted it over the goal line—and it moved. Hornung immediately got 16 on a plunge through a left-side hole. Taylor got another 13 on 3 straight rushes. Then Starr hit Hornung for 8, and Taylor swept left out of bounds for another 8: Ball on the Eagle 35.

Then Starr hit Taylor for 15. Next Starr hit Hornung for 8. Then Starr hit Knafelc for 6. The ball now was on the Eagle 7 with time quickly running out—44 seconds. Starr ran a play and was nailed for no gain, but Philadelphia was called for off side. Accepting the penalty would have given Green Bay a poorer angle for a field goal, so it declined. Hornung tried from the 14 from a still relatively difficult angle—and missed.

So the half ended 10-6 Eagles, for all of Green Bay's threatening.

Early in the second half, Green Bay moved the ball again for 2 quick first downs on bursts by Taylor and Hornung—but lost the ball on the Eagle 30 on downs when Taylor was stopped just short. And here the Eagles moved the ball well to a quick first down on the Packer 5 (McDonald got 33 on a slant, Walston got 25 more on the 2 big plays), only to have Johnny Symank intercept Van Brocklin's pass in the end zone. That gave the Packers possession on their 20—and the Packers then went on to score on an 80-yard drive that included the most spectacular play of the contest.

Stopped with fourth and 10 on the Packer 20 after 3 straight incomplete passes, McGee dropped back to punt but didn't. Instead, he saw that Philadelphia didn't have a rush on. "Everybody backed up and so I took off. I held the ball long enough to see them all turn tail . . . it definitely wasn't a gamble—I could see ten yards. As it was, I could see touchdown if I'd gone the other way (I saw about four blockers ahead of me and their two safety men—looking up as if they expected the punt) . . . I cut to the inside when I should have cut to the outside and I'd have been gone all the way." Lombardi pointed out that it was not just an extemporaneous play, but that a fake punt had always been worked on in practice and that in this case "everybody backed off so he took off." Philadelphia Coach Shaw noted that defensive end Joe Robb was "a little careless" on the play.

At any rate, McGee raced 35 big yards to the Eagle 46 on the fourth-down punt play. On the play, Hornung—a great blocker besides being a smashing runner—was belted hard by Bednarik and suffered a pinched nerve in his shoulder that took him out of the game. It was a critical play.

Hornung's replacement, Tom Moore, immediately lost 5 yards on the next play—and then dropped a Starr pass on the next. Knafelc then took still another pass for 17 to a first down on the

34 on a big third-down play. Finally Moore grabbed a dozen yards on a first down play to the 22. A bang by Taylor got 4, then Moore got 8 inside left end, and it was first down on the 10. After Taylor got 3 more, Starr pitched to McGee for a TD. Hornung converted the PAT, and it was 13-10.

The time left in the game was 13:07.

And now came the most decisive play in the contest. Green Bay had to kick off, but with an average runback Philadelphia would probably be left well in its own territory to initiate its comeback.

The runback, though, was extraordinary: A scintillating dash by Dean from his 3 all the way to the Packer 39, taking advantage of crushing blocks. Instead of having long yardage to negotiate with time beginning to ebb, Philadelphia was in a charging position with plenty of time.

And the Eagles charged.

A Packer holding penalty cost them yardage on the first play, and 2 rushes by Dean and Barnes moved the ball to another first down on the 20. Van Brocklin was thrown for a loss back to the 27 on the next play, but he fired right back with a pop-pass to Barnes for 13, and when Barnes carried for 5 on the next play it was first and goal on the 9-yard line. A smash by Dean up the middle got to the 5, and when he swung wide around left end he was in the end zone. Walston booted the placement, it was 17-13 with 9 and a half minutes remaining.

The Packers started to move after the kickoff but McGee fumbled a first-down pass on the Eagle 48, and Bednarik pounced on the ball. It was another big play for Philadelphia.

Green Bay forced a punt in short order, however—but now had to start out on its 12. Shortly a pass to Knafelc missed on a third-and-2 situation, and the Packers once more had to punt the ball away. As Starr lamented in the locker room later, "We lost it when we missed on that pass to Gary with four and a half minutes to play; if we'd hit on that, we would have been all right—but as it was, it gave them a chance to kill more time."

McGee got off a tremendous boot, the ball rolling dead on the Eagle 25. Again Green Bay held, made Philly kick, and Van Brocklin's punt was run back 6 yards by Lew Carpenter to his 35.

This was obviously the Packers' last chance, for a scant minute and a half remained to play. Starr used that time magnificently. First he passed to Taylor for 5, then to Moore for 4, and on third down sent Taylor wide to the left and out of bounds for 9 big yards to the Eagle 47—also stopping the clock. Then Starr hit Knafelc for 17 to the 30—with only 30 seconds left. He went to Boyd Dowler in the end zone on the next play; Dowler was bumped by the defense and complained vigorously of "interference"—but the pass was incomplete and no penalty was called. When Knafelc took the next pass for 8 to the 22, there was time for only 1 more play.

That play, as noted, went to Taylor on a short flip at the scrimmage line, but it was finally stopped 9 yards from the goal line as Bednarik wrestled the bullish fullback down.

Starr had run off 7 plays in less than 90 seconds, moved his team from his 35 to the 9, but just couldn't quite beat the clock.

Philadelphia, as noted, had set up an umbrella defense to guard against long-gainers. Said Shaw, who had come out of virtual retirement after the 1958 season for "three more years" and promised retirement now: "We put an extra halfback on defense at the end and took the linebacker out since we knew they would be throwing the ball." Shaw's defensive tactics proved extremely sound throughout the game. He used a stunting defense all the way. "If we'd played them honest, they'd have handled us pretty well; they know right where you are. So we showed them a 4-3, then changed at the snap of the ball with the defensive end moving in tight and the linebacker taking his spot. We had to do it—they're a pretty damned good blocking team."

The silvery-haired coach acknowledged that his team was "pretty tense" at the start, but as time went on "relaxed a little." Stopping the Packers early in the game "helped us, it made us believe we could do the job," he observed.

Van Brocklin, always an outspoken locker room man, said that the Eagles "didn't really play up to potential; we really didn't play very good football . . . but that's the kind of a team we are—we play as hard as we have to. Defensively I think we did a hell of a good job, but we didn't do too well on offense."

The morose Packers, almost to a man, felt that "the better team lost," although also acknowledging Eagle ability.

PHILADELPHIA EAGLES VS. GREEN BAY PACKERS, 1960

For the Eagles, victory meant $5,116 to each man. The losing Packers got $3,105.

The Scoring:

Philadelphia	0	10	0	7	—	17
Green Bay	3	3	0	7	—	13

GB—FG Hornung 20
GB—FG Hornung 23
Phil.—McDonald 35, Van Brocklin pass (Walston kick)
Phil.—FG Walston 15
GB—McGee 7, Starr pass (Hornung kick)
Phil.—Dean 5, run (Walston kick)

The Statistics:

	Phil.	GB
First downs	13	22
Rushing yardage	99	223
Passing yardage	197	178
Passes	9-20	21-35
Own passes intercepted	1	0
Punting	6-40	5-45
Fumbles lost	2	1
Penalties	0-0	4-27

XIV

NEW YORK GIANTS VS. NOTRE DAME ALL STARS
(Game played December 14, 1930)

NEW YORK, N.Y. (Dec. 15, 1930)—The name of Notre Dame proved to be a magnet in attracting a shivering crowd of nearly 50,000 to the Polo Grounds yesterday. But the halo of invincibility that has encircled the crowned heads of Notre Dame's all-conquering football teams of the past 2 years was totally obliterated as the Notre Dame All Stars went down to a crushing 22-0 defeat at the hands of Benny Friedman and his New York Professional Football Giants on the bleak, frostbitten field.

With the great crowd looking on in bewilderment, Friedman and his husky mates made a shambles of the charity game, played for the benefit of the unemployed and the needy. They played Knute Rockne's outstanding players from the days of the Four Horsemen.

Conspicuous among the crowd who paid $112,000 at the gate were former Governor Alfred E. Smith, Mayor Jimmy Walker, and Knute Rockne, huddled in blankets on the sidelines.

From start to finish there was never any doubt about the outcome of the game—the Giants had the South Benders utterly at their mercy. Until the Giants withdrew their regulars in the second half, they had ripped and passed their way down the field almost at will. Friedman, the former Michigan quarterback, projected his passes in his own inimitable fashion and carried the ball twice for touchdowns and was the outstanding gainer on the field with 69 total yards rushing. Both of Friedman's touchdowns were made in the second quarter, one of them on a bull-like charge through center for 20 yards leaving half a dozen former Notre Dame men strewn across the field.

Another touchdown by Campbell on a 22-yard pass from Moran in the third period, a safety scored in the opening period when Harry Stuhldreher was thrown behind his own goal line in attempting to get off a pass, and 2 placement kicks for extra points, one each by Friedman and Moran, accounted for the Giants' 22 points.

The All Stars were never within striking distance of the Giants' goal line. The closest they ever got with the ball, in fact, was 51 yards away in the second period.

Probably never before has such a galaxy of shining lights of the gridiron been brought together at one time as upon the hardened surface of the Polo Grounds that day. In the parade were the Four Horsemen of 1924, the most famous backfield in football history—Stuhldreher, Don Miller, "Sleepy" Jim Crowley, and Elmer Layden. In front of them at the start of the game were 5 of the Seven Mules behind whom they rode to a national championship—Adam Walsh, center; Joe Bach and Noble Kizer, guards; Rip Miller, tackle; and Ed Hunsinger, end, although not all of these were regular starters in 1924. Following in the procession at the start of the second period were 5 members of the stalwart line that was the main strength of Notre Dame's unbeaten 1929 team—Jack Cannon, John Law, Tim Moynihan, Ted Twomey, and Joe Vezie—helping again to open up holes that were all too few for Elder, the hero of Notre Dame's victory over Army in 1929, and John Gebert.

Still more came in their wake as Rockne sought to put together a combination that could capture the vital spark to offset the handicap of lack of intensive training and practice together. Frank Carideo, the almost unanimous choice for All-American quarterback this year and one of the brainiest field generals the game has produced; Bucky O'Connor, hero of the Southern California game a week ago; Hunk Anderson, line coach at South Bend; and Jack Chevigny, an outstanding back of 1928—all of these and others were rushed into the fray in the effort to break the Giants' hammerlock on the All Stars' offense.

From the opposite side of the field came Friedman and Red Cagle, the latter to renew his rivalry with the Rockne men of the Army days, and a host of others whose names did not mean so much to an Eastern crowd but whose exploits by the end of the afternoon won the stamp of merit.

The Four Horsemen played through the first quarter with the exception of Crowley, who was injured and replaced by Elder midway in the first period, and were totally helpless. They advanced the ball only 5 yards while losing 17 in the quarter. In the parlance of Broadway, the backfield that had ridden rough-shod over all opposition was taken for a ride toward their own goal line.

All of the other All Star backs were almost equally helpless, except for a 7-yard dash by Elder on his first play and a 12-yard run by Enright in the second period. The Giants' forward wall charged with such fury and power that the opposing line was helpless, and the passing attack was completely destroyed.

It was hard for the spectator to believe his eyes to see so much ground gained through linemen who were so adamant in their undergraduate days as were Walsh, Kizer, and Anderson. In justice to the All Stars, they were in no condition to hold their own with a strapping, perfectly trained outfit that had been in competition for months, with its attack perfectly coordinated and every man knowing his job to the letter. Hastily banded together, without benefit of the hard exercise so necessary for perfect condition, and with only a few days of preparation together in signal drill, it is no wonder that they were overpowered by their heavy opponents. Their play was faltering and uncertain throughout the game. Many of them were summoned from their coaching posts and had only a few hours in which to familiarize themselves with plays that they had not executed since their college days. Rip Miller, the Navy line coach, joined the team only the Saturday night before.

All of this is put down as a deserved consideration for the handicap under which the All Stars were playing in lending their services for a worthy cause. It is not meant to detract in any way from the splendid performance of the Giants, whose work on both the offense and defense was a revelation to many. The notion had been entertained in some quarters that the professional brand of football is of the laissez-faire variety and that the paid player does not throw himself into the game with the spirit and inspiration of the college player. There isn't a team that has played any fiercer, more intense and more teeth-jolting a brand of football than Friedman and his mates displayed yesterday. The Giants, as they performed, were qualified to give any college team of the season all the opposition it could want.

Undaunted by the reputation of the players they were meeting, the Giants launched an attack in the first few minutes of the game that carried 59 yards to the All Stars' 11-yard line. Friedman threw passes to Sedbrook for 25 and 16 yards. The All Stars' defense stiffened, and on fourth down Friedman threw a pass into the end zone that was knocked down.

Taking the ball the All Stars found themselves powerless with it. Crowley was thrown for a 10-yard loss by Morris Badgro in trying to get off a pass. They then lost ground on an exchange of kicks and were penalized 5 yards on an offside penalty, leaving the ball on the 7-yard line.

Stuhldreher, the former quarterback of the Four Horsemen, dropped back to his own goal line, but before he could pass or kick, Bill Owen was on top of him like a flash to drive him across the goal line, where he was dropped by Badgro for a safety.

Starting near the end of the first period and extending into the first part of the second period, the Giants gobbled up 51 yards in 11 plays for a touchdown. Friedman smashed through from the middle of the field to Notre Dame's 37-yard line, and then tossed a forward pass over the center to Badgro, which brought the ball to the Notre Dame 15-yard line as the first period ended.

Friedman sliced through the short side of the Notre Dame line for a first down on the 3, and after Notre Dame had made a great stand and repulsed 2 line smashes by Sedbrook, Friedman hurled himself over a pile of players for a touchdown. Friedman tried a pass for the extra point. Wiberg caught it outside the goal line but Chevigny downed him before he could get over.

After Chevigny had been thrown for a 10-yard loss by Badgro, Carideo got away a short punt and Friedman brought it back to the Notre Dame 35-yard line. Wiberg tossed a pass to Sedbrook, who was stopped on the Notre Dame 20. From there, Friedman cut through the line, shook himself free of 3 Notre Dame tacklers who seemed to have him nailed, and went 20 yards for the touchdown. He kicked the placement for the extra point.

By this time the crowd had begun to lose some of its interest, for it was apparent that the Giants could not be stopped, and in the third period the All Stars were almost pathetic.

With Elder, Stuhldreher, O'Connor, and Enright in the back field, the All Stars took the ball on their 32-yard line, and in rapid succession Elder lost 4, Stuhldreher 9, and Elder 13 more—with

Hoot Gibson, Giant tackle, breaking through on the last as Elder tried to throw a pass. Elder was forced to kick from his goal line, sending it to his own 42-yard line.

Cagle's run for 15 yards to the Notre Dame 27 started the Giants on their way to their other touchdown in the third period. It was the longest run in Cagle's professional career. Then Dale Burnett and Cagle jammed through for a first down. Burnett sliced through the Notre Dame line for 10 yards, but the Giants were offside on the play and penalized 5 yards. Bill Morgan then threw a pass to Campbell, who took it over the goal line. Moran kicked the placement for the extra point.

Both teams had their reserves in the game for the final period, and neither was able to make any progress. The ball was in All-Star territory for the entire final period as they gained only 4 yards for the quarter.

The Giants were a closely welded, smoothly working football team through the afternoon. They wasted no motion, they knew their business and carried out their assignments so expertly that there seemed to be no exertion on their part. They had speed, they started with a dash and turned like flashes.

But the greatest difference was Benny Friedman. His passes to Sedbrook, a receiver of remarkable speed, and Campbell and Badgro were masterpieces of control and accuracy. Friedman's deception in ball handling, his quick slants through the Notre Dame line, and his total generalship were football skill at its best.

The Scoring:

New York	2	13	7	0	—	22
All Stars	0	0	0	0	—	0

Touchdowns: (NY) Friedman (2), Campbell

Extra Points: (NY) Friedman, Moran

Safety: Stuhldreher (tackled by Badgro)

137

XV

DALLAS TEXANS VS. HOUSTON OILERS
(Game played December 23, 1962)

HOUSTON, TEXAS (December 24, 1962)—They fought through 4 full quarters of football and couldn't settle anything. So they played another quarter—and still couldn't decide anything. And so they went at it for almost 3 more minutes before finally determining who would rule the American Football League yesterday.

Dallas won.

Here in Jeppesen Stadium on Sunday, the Dallas Texans doggedly outlasted Houston's Oilers in the wearying sixth quarter of "Sudden Death"—although there was little suddenness about it. The score was 20-17.

Only one other overtime game has been played in professional football, the historic Baltimore-New York playoff of 1958, which the Colts won, 23-17. This game lasted almost 10 minutes longer, the 2 Texas teams playing for an astounding 77 minutes and 54 seconds before 37,981 enthralled fans. Victory was achieved on a 24-yard field goal by rookie Tom Brooker.

Before the ball split the uprights, the teams had been struggling for more than 3 hours since the 2 P. M. kickoff. And each seemingly had its opportunities to put it away.

Dallas had gotten off to a 17-0 lead in the first half and appeared destined for victory. But Houston staged a spirited comeback in the second half and scored an equalizing 17. With 3 minutes left in the game, the Oilers had a field goal blocked to force overtime.

After winning the flip of the coin to start the overtime, Dallas incredibly blew its option by misinforming the referee of its wishes, and thereby put itself in the hole at the outset. Eventually a pass interception averted the initial Houston threat. Then, as the fifth quarter was running out, Houston disdained a long field-goal try and attempted to move the ball closer for an easier kick, only to have another pass intercepted. And not only did that theft

139

thwart the Oilers, but the runback gave Dallas a midfield position—and barely 3 minutes later the Texans had moved within range of Brooker's foot.

This was no humdrum ball game!

Although Brooker's winning field goal is the play that will go on the books as the decisive one, the most discussed aspect of this memorable contest wasn't actually a play at all. It was the boner between the end of the regulation game and the start of overtime. And it was a beaut. Dallas offensive captain Abner Haynes had correctly called the flip of the coin to decide options—but when it came to announcing the Dallas desires, he simply forgot the carefully thought-out "flip plan." Both teams were aghast.

Each squad had made its plans for the coin-flip, for on this muddy field (hardly "turf" on the virtually grassless surface after the season's pounding) and in a light drizzle coupled with 12- to 14-mile winds, the opportunity to begin play in the most advantageous way was obviously critical in sudden death. And Dallas had that opportunity.

As Dallas Coach Hank Stram reasoned, "We'd be in better position to kick off and try to hold them deep in their territory. We were going good defensively but we weren't moving the ball and we weren't punting good. So we wanted to kick off and we wanted to take the wind." Stram's instructions were that they won the toss, Haynes was to opt for kicking with the wind. Stram reasoned that with the wind at his back, the Oilers' George Blanda would probably boot the ball out of the park and make Dallas start out on its 20 against the wind. If the overtime went the way the last part of the regular game had gone, the Texans would shortly have to punt and thereby give Houston great field position. So the Dallas theory was that it would be better to kick off and trust that the stalwart Texan line would hold . . . after which, with the wind at its back, it would wind up with a favorable attacking position.

So Haynes was supposed to choose the north goal and the following wind (which would have meant that Houston would probably receive). Instead, he said that he chose to kick off. Thus Houston astonishingly was given its choice of goals and naturally picked the north one—and the wind that was so vital.

140

Houston players were shocked. As quarterback Blanda remarked later with a wondering shake of his head, "we thought they were crazy." Dallas players were equally incredulous but could only fume inwardly at the goof. Eventually, the miscall didn't hurt because the game took so long. Dallas had the wind with it when Brooker had his shot at the deciding field goal. But before then, it seemed a disastrous slipup.

Dallas had to kick off into the wind (just what Stram did not want to do), and Houston started out on its 25. Blanda immediately connected to Willard Dewveall for 9 yards to the 34: second and 1. But instead of doing the expected—running—the cagey Blanda twice tried short flips to running back Billy Cannon. Both were weak, both missed. And Houston had to punt.

Cannon later lamented, "If there was any turning point, it was my dropping those two passes on that one-yard situation." E. J. Holub was on top of him both times, but the throws probably were not the best either. As to second-guesses about why the Oilers didn't run for the yard, Cannon staunchly defended the calls. "All we needed was a yard, and the play was open for a yard. You can't second-guess a man that's called as many games as George; if I catch the ball, he's a hero."

But Dallas was unable to move the ball and it too had to kick—a weak 27-yarder to the Oiler 45. And so again Houston had field position.

This time it was an interception that snuffed out the threat, Johnny Robinson picking one off from his safety slot and lugging it back 13 yards to the Houston 47. But again Dallas was kept from going anywhere and had to punt—only this time the kick rolled dead on the Oiler 12.

If fans thought Houston was in a deep hole, they were mistaken. For 3 times Blanda peppered the Texan defenses with precision passes to Dewveall, to Charley Hennigan, and to Bob McLeod for 12, 9, and 15 while mixing in rushing plays that advanced them to the Dallas 35.

Now Houston was within field-goal range, for Blanda is a 40-yard booter. But when a running play lost a yard, the Oilers went to the air. Defensive end Bill Hull dropped back to snag the pass for an interception on the 27 and scooted back to midfield. Two plays later, the first extra quarter ended.

Blanda later wistfully commented, "If I'd called a hook-in instead of a down-and-out, it would have gone." Hull admitted that "they really had me mixed up there for a while," explaining that since the Texans were rushing only 3 men, he was dropping back and became a fourth linebacker "and felt pretty strange back there." But he correctly diagnosed the play, saw the ball coming "right at me—it surprised me, but I wasn't about to drop the ball," and took off. His idea of running it back all the way was balked when he was dropped at midfield by intended receiver Hennigan.

Stram had set up a daring 3-4 defense just the opposite of that normally used, shooting 3 men in and keeping Hull back as a linebacker at his end position. The newly conceived defense was designed to stop Houston's vaunted power game and short-passing attack—and it obviously worked well. The Dallas secondary played a basic zone defense, which forced Blanda to stick largely to short shots; and although 23 of 46 passes were completed for good yardage (261 yards), there were also 5 costly interceptions.

When the second overtime period began, Dallas began to move. It was Jack Spikes, injured most of the season and a sub for flashy rookie Curtis McClinton when he did return, who was the spark. In fact, he would up winning press-box acclaim as the game's outstanding player. First Spikes took Lennie Dawson's flat pass for a gain to the Houston 38 and his team's deepest penetration since the first half. Next, anticipating a blitz, Dawson shot Spikes through left tackle, and the big fullback busted through to the Houston 19. Then Dawson went to Spikes a third time, flipping the ball to him near the goal line. Spikes tripped when turning to catch it, and the pass fell incomplete.

Now Dawson (and Stram) decided to forego a try for a TD in favor of a close-up shot at a field goal; and the next 2 plays were used simply to set up a kick smack in front of the goalposts while the frustrated Oilers could only hit and hope for a fumble. With the ball on the 17, young Brooker was waved in.

The husky rookie later recalled, sitting dazedly in the locker room, "Lenny [Dawson] told everybody to be quiet in the huddle because it might make me nervous . . . we called time out so I could clean the mud from my shoe . . . then I just waited and kept my eyes on the ground . . . I knew Lenny would place the ball right for me because he's the best at that—I always get a solid shot at the target . . . I never took my eyes off the ground until after the kick; then I looked up and saw the ball going through the uprights." And so it ended, 20-17, after 77:54.

The "longest day" in football.

The Houston loss was particularly bitter for the largely Oiler rooters, who sat through a game that saw their favorites trail 0—17 and then rally to tie 17-all and generally hold the upper hand over the latter stages of the marathon. But they saw a game that perhaps never will be surpassed for length and overall grippingness. At the finish, both winners and losers alike were "dead." As, indeed, were the spectators.

With those 0-17 and 17-0 scores for the 2 teams in each half, it was obviously a game of changing tempo. Dallas had the early momentum. Houston made only one real threat. It drove 52 yards to the Texan 5-yard line for a first down, but then was thrown back. With third down on the 9, Blanda pegged down the middle but Holub intercepted. He scampered back to his 43, and that, on its own, not only ended the Oiler threat but also gave Dallas position.

From there Dawson guided the Texans to the Houston 8 with a mixture of rushes and passes, before being forced to settle for a 15-yard field goal by Brooker. Four and a half minutes remained in the opening quarter.

The next time it got the ball, Dallas went all the way. One big play came when Spikes slashed along the sideline for 33 yards and then was handed an extra 15 on a face-mask penalty against the Oilers. With second and 1 on the 28, Dawson switched to the air and hit Haynes around the 20 for a TD strike. It was a quick 80-yard march, making it 10-0 early in the second quarter.

Later in the period, another Blanda pass was intercepted—this one by Dave Grayson, who raced from midfield to the Oiler 29. Seven plays later, with McClinton and Haynes doing the work, the ball was in the end zone via the latter's 2-yard smash through the left side of the line: 17-0, and less than 4 minutes left in the half.

Up to now, apart from its opening sally, Houston had done

nothing—but a 48-yard kickoff runback by Bobby Jancik put the Oilers at midfield, and from there they penetrated to the 25 before a couple of Blanda passes were dropped to end the threat. It had been a discouraging first half for Houston, which couldn't help remembering its 31-7 licking here earlier in the campaign.

But after the intermission, the Oilers looked like a different ball club—most particularly because Blanda began connecting with his receivers. They swept 67 yards to a TD in just 6 plays after the second-half kickoff, with Dewveall making 3 key catches of 24, 12, and 15 yards—the last one as he tumbled into the end zone.

Later in the period a fumble by Haynes gave Houston possession on the Dallas 20 for another great chance, but it was frittered away on an interception by Robinson. And so it went into the fourth quarter at 17-7.

Four minutes after the final period began, Houston got within touchdown range after marching from its 43 to the Texan 15 before being thrown back—but at least it came away with something when Blanda booted a field goal from the 31. So now it was 17-10, and there was still ample time for more points.

And Houston got those points with some 6 minutes still to go. Again guiding his charges niftily, Blanda produced a drive for half the field with another masterful mixing of offensive weapons that ended with Charley Tolar belting in from a yard out. When Blanda kicked the PAT, it was 17-all.

The Oilers got one more crack at scoring when another feeble Dallas kick rolled dead on the Texan 41 with time running out. But Dallas got tough, forced Houston into a fourth-down situation on the 35, and it was time for another field-goal try. Three minutes remained.

Blanda dropped back to the 42, and the other 21 men prepared to defend or block. One of them was Sherrill Headrick, Dallas' fine linebacker. "I wasn't even going to rush on the kick," he disclosed in the locker room later. "I never have before. But I took a step and saw a hole in the middle, so I decided to blast in there; I went right through two blockers who probably knew I never rushed and were thinking about blocking somebody else. I stuck my hand up, and suddenly the ball was back there on the ground."

Headrick's blocking of the kick ended the last threat by either team during the regulation time. And little anyone could know that over 20 more minutes would elapse after that play before another field goal—this one successful—would finally end it all.

Including Houston's 2-year championship reign in the new AFL.

The Scoring:

Dallas	3	14	0	0	0	3	—	20
Houston	0	0	7	10	0	0	—	17

Dal.—FG Brooker 15
Dal.—Haynes 28, Dawson pass (Brooker kick)
Dal.—Haynes 2, run (Brooker kick)
Hou.—Dewveall 15, Blanda pass (Blanda kick)
Hou.—FG Blanda 31
Hou.—Tolar 1, run (Blanda kick)
Dal.—FG Brooker 25

The Statistics:

	Dal.	Hou.
First downs	19	21
Rushing yardage	199	98
Passing yardage	88	261
Passes	9-14	23-46
Own passes intercepted	0	5
Punting	8-31	3-39
Fumbles lost	1	0
Penalties	42	50

145

XVI

DALLAS COWBOYS VS. GREEN BAY PACKERS
(Game played January 1, 1967)

DALLAS, TEXAS, (Jan. 2, 1967)—In the fiercely proud tradition of Lombardi-honed teams, the Green Bay Packers came up with a tremendous goal-line stand and the "big play" to avert an almost certain tie with Dallas in the National Football League's championship game here yesterday.

Indeed, they came up with 4 great plays in the last 2 minutes to thwart a stadium-rocking Cowboy comeback and doom Dallas to a frustrating 34-27 defeat. The Cowboys had been down 34-20 but had rallied brilliantly late in the fourth quarter to threaten to force the game into sudden death. With just 1:52 remaining to play, they had forged a first down on the Packer 2-yard line and were seemingly in full cry.

But Green Bay grimly held for 3 savage thrusts and then made one last inspired play to save its victory and claim its second consecutive NFL title.

That big play, with fourth and 2 and just over 30 seconds to go, was magnificently executed by Packer linebacker Dave Robinson. He diagnosed it; he defended against it superbly. With the clock running and a scant 2 yards to go, Dallas decided on a rollout, and quarterback Don Meredith took the snap and headed to his right. It was a fatal choice of plays. Robinson, playing the left side of the line, thrust end Bob Hayes aside, eluded guard Leon Donohue, and got to Meredith near the sidelines. Putting the clamps on him, he forced the Cowboy to fling a wobbly, fluttering pass into the air (actually, it was a great pressure effort by Meredith in even being able to get the ball away at all), and Tom Brown intercepted to end it. Twenty-eight seconds were left.

Even Dallas acknowledged the expertise that Robinson showed. Said backfield coach Ermal Allen, "He made the play himself. We'd never run that to the right out of a Brown-left formation, so he hadn't seen it on the films or been told to watch for it. He just reacted properly."

147

In the dressing room after the game, Robinson described his actions: "It looked like a run to me at first. I played it for the run—in fact, I have to. And Meredith made a good play himself; a lot of quarterbacks would have eaten the ball. I had hold of him and I had his left arm completely paralyzed and I had his right arm at the elbow so he just flipped it with his wrist. I thought it was a good move on his part."

Sitting nearby as he wearily but elatedly undressed, Brown elaborated further on the play: "I had to do something after [Frank] Clarke got behind me for a touchdown and I got called for interference on that third-down play at the end. He had to throw it—it was fourth down. He did the only thing he could under the circumstances. Hayes was on my left and Clarke was on my right . . . I think Meredith saw a white jersey and just threw it . . . I think he threw it sidearm and it was just wobbling—and I just moved over." He added: "That ball . . . looked, oh, so nice!"

A gloomy Dallas Coach Tom Landry defended the call in this way: "You can run if you want to take a chance with fourth and two . . . we decided to go to a fake run and rollout, which has worked for us a lot this year—but it didn't this time." He added wistfully: "We had the momentum at the end; if we'd scored, we would have beaten them in overtime."

That a great defensive play should climax the game was anything but typical of what had gone before in the preceding 59 and a half minutes. For this was a spectacular offensive show for the 74,152 spectators gathered in the Cotton Bowl in ideal 52-degree weather. Illustrative of the wide-open game the two teams played are these figures:

> 61 points
> 42 first downs
> 785 total yards

And considerably more than a thrill a minute!

Green Bay had struck with startling suddenness for two touchdowns in the opening minutes of the game (2 within literally seconds of each other); then yielded to 2 Dallas drives for 14-all *still* in the first quarter; regained the lead once more, only to have the Cowboys rally again and close to within a point at 21-20; and then drove for 2 more TDs to build up its ultimately impregnable 34-20 margin, which withstood Dallas' last gallant charge.

148

Surprisingly, Dallas outgained Green Bay 418 yards to 367 and controlled the ball 73 plays to 58—yet lost. However, it was the Packers' failure to convert the extra point after their fifth touchdown that produced the tension. The point margin going into those final frantic minutes would have been 8 rather than 7, and the outcome would have been almost certain, with even a last Cowboy TD unable to tie the score.

At the time, with a 34-20 lead and the game already in the final quarter, the missed extra point did not seem unduly significant. With a chance to ice the game in this balmy weather, the Packers' Don Chandler barely got the ball off the ground; Bob Lilly got official credit for blocking it, and so instead of a 15-point spread, it was 14, and two TDs could at least force overtime. It gave Dallas life.

Instantly aware that they had been given a reprieve from almost certain defeat, the Cowboys fired up with verve—and the needed execution. The ball game thereafter was theirs . . . except for that ultimate Packer stand.

Mel Renfro ran the kickoff back 26 yards to his 29 to get things started. Thereafter it was Meredith doing things with the ball on 5 straight plays. First he hit Pettis Norman for 8. Second, he took it up the middle himself for 5. Third, he overthrew a pass. Fourth, he flipped to Dan Reeves, who fumbled—but Meredith recovered, but for a 10-yard loss back to the 32. Fifth, he passed again, this time to Clarke, who got beyond the secondary and went flying all the way for a 68-yard touchdown. Danny Villanueva kicked the extra point, and in just 5 plays Dallas was suddenly very much a threat. Now, indeed, that missed extra point loomed as the possible game-decider.

Now, though, Dallas had to kick to Green Bay, and if the Badgerland team could manage a couple of first downs they would just about be home free. But they couldn't, not against a suddenly inflamed Cowboy defense.

Herb Adderley ran the kickoff back 13 to his 28, and Bart Starr immediately threw to big tight end Marv Fleming for 18 to the 46. "Ahhhhhh," sighed the few Packer fans.

But thereafter it was disaster for Green Bay. Dave Edwards crunched Starr for a loss of 8 yards on the next play; Willie Townes deflected his pass on the next; and on the next Lee Roy

149

Jordan sliced in to drop Jim Taylor for a loss of 7 more yards after the Packer fullback had taken a swing pass from Starr. So a punt was forced, and with an average kick Dallas could anticipate getting the ball somewhere around its 30.

But an aroused Dallas line forced a rushed kick by Chandler, and the ball angled out of bounds after a mere 16 yards. Suddenly Dallas had possession on the Packer 47 instead of deep in its own territory. And suddenly the game had changed.

Meredith hit Clarke for 21 "biggies" right off the bat on first down to put the ball on the 26, and the game indeed had changed. And when Don Perkins belted the middle for 4, it was second down on the 22 and the 2-minute warning sounded. Again Meredith went to the air, trying to find Clarke in the right corner of the end zone, but Brown was on him—and he stopped a sure touchdown the only way possible, by interfering with the Cowboy receiver. It was a costly penalty, putting the ball on the 2-yard line—and with 1:52 still left in the game.

Now the Cowboys could really "work" on their foes.

They shot Reeves into the line for one, and the distance was halved. Then Meredith sought to fool the Packers—massed for an anticipated up-the-middle smash again—by calling a rollout himself, flipping a short pass to Norman. Norman dropped the ball, but that was incidental; what really mattered was that a Dallas lineman was called for illegal procedure, and after the 5-yard penalty it was no longer a yard to go but 6. Albeit still with 3 plays to get those 6. Now, though, the Packers had a little room in which to "work"—although the impetus still belonged to Dallas.

Now Meredith went to a swing pass, trying to hit Reeves on the left. No good. Next Meredith sought to make connection with Norman—and the husky tight end grabbed the ball near the goal line. It could well have gone for a touchdown, but Brown desperately flung himself at Norman and forced him down as the Cowboy struggled toward the line. The play was ruled dead 2 yards short.

Whereupon Meredith did his roll, Robinson did his thing, and Brown made up for what he called his earlier "boo-boo" by spearing the wounded-duck pass for the game-settling interception.

150

GAME 16
Dallas Cowboys vs.
Green Bay Packers
January 1, 1967

Packer end Boyd
Dowler (86) takes a 16-
yard touchdown pass
from Bart Starr at the
start of the third
quarter. *(U.P.I.)*

Elijah Pitts (22), Green Bay's replacement for Paul Hornung, races 32 yards into Cowboy territory in the first period. *(U.P.I.)*

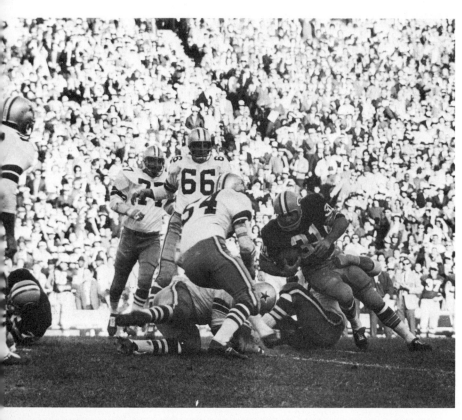

Jim Taylor (31) goes absolutely nowhere as he is brought down from behind by Bob Lilly of Dallas. *(U.P.I.)*

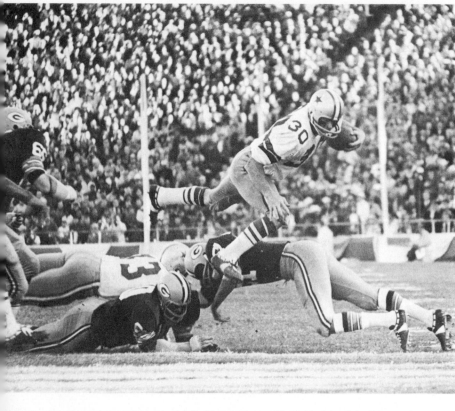

Cowboy Dan Reeves (30) leaps for a 4-yard gain just before the end of the first half. *(U.P.I.)*

GAME 17
Green Bay Packers vs.
Baltimore Colts
December 26, 1965

Don Shinnick (66) of
the Colts races into the
end zone for a
touchdown after
recovering a fumble by
Packers' Bill Anderson.
Starr (15), lying on his
back, was injured on the
play and removed from
the game. The play was
the very first scrimmage
of the game.
(U.P.I.)

Don Chandler (34)
kicks the winning field
goal from the 25-yard
line after 13 minutes
and 39 seconds of a
sudden-death overtime.
(U.P.I.)

Billy Ray Smith (74) gets to Green Bay quarterback Zeke Bratkowski with a vengeance in the second period. *(U.P.I.)*

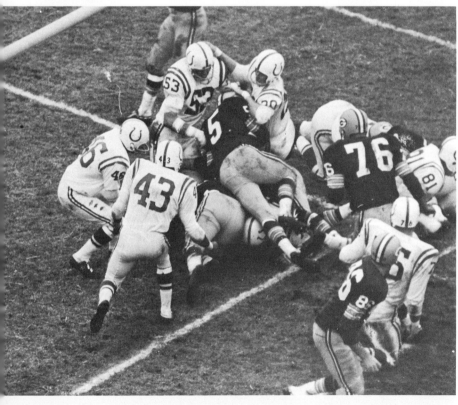

Paul Hornung (5) goes into the end zone for Green Bay's only touchdown from the 1-yard line. *(U.P.I.)*

GAME 18
Green Bay Packers vs.
New York Giants
December 11, 1938

Tuffy Leemans scores
the first Giant
touchdown in the first
period. *(U.P.I.)*

Clarke Hinkle (far
right) cuts through the
center of the Giant line
for 1 yard in the second
period. Two plays later,
Hinkle went over for
the touchdown. *(U.P.I.)*

Clark Hinkle stops for no gain as Cecil Isbell (17) and Bud Svendsen (53) look on.

Leemans (4) starts around his right end but runs into a stone wall. Green Bay was penalized 15 yards for unnecessary roughness on the play. *(U.P.I.)*

All Starr had to do thereafter was flop on the ball for 2 plays and it was over.

Actually, the game had begun in an equally sensational manner. And continued that way throughout all 60 minutes.

After Donny Anderson had run the opening kickoff back 22 yards to his 24, the Packers struck swiftly. Elijah Pitts, in there for super-ace Paul Hornung, still injury-bothered, burst through right tackle for 32 yards on the first play from scrimmage, and the Packers were in Dallas territory. Five more plays netted 2 first downs and then, with second and 7 on the Cowboy 17, Starr found Pitts on a pass who eluded 3 Texans to go all the way.

With Chandler's PAT, a quick 7-0.

It would quickly be 14-0. Only a dozen seconds were needed to boost the score to that spread—and without a Packer play. Chandler kicked off. Renfro fumbled (Brown and hulking Gale Gillingham—both rookies—hit him). Jim Grabowski (another rookie) scooped up the ball and dashed into the end zone. Six points. Then 7 on Chandler's place-kick: 14-0, and still not a Dallas play.

But Dallas, still not discouraged, starting on its 35 after the kickoff, swept 65 yards for a TD in 13 plays, with Reeves ripping off right tackle for the last 3. Villanueva made it 14-7.

And it didn't take long to tie it up. Dallas kicked off, held, and in just 5 plays moved 59 yards to score again, this time with Perkins plunging through a hole off right guard and blasting free for 23 yards to the goal line.

But if this seemed to indicate that the game was going Dallas' way, it wasn't so. Three plays after the kickoff netted Green Bay 64 yards and a 21-14 lead. The payoff was a 51-yard strike from Starr to Carroll Dale—completed only because defender Cornell Green misjudged the ball. He was "on" the underthrown ball all the way for a sure block or interception, misestimated it, and the ball somehow landed in Dale's hands.

That took care of the first-half touchdowns—but not the scoring. Stopped on the Packer 4-yard line midway through the second period, Villanueva dropped back to the 11 and booted a field goal, narrowing the score to 21-17. The kick capped a 12-play march that gobbled up 72 yards following the kickoff.

159

A later field-goal try by Chandler from the Dallas 30 was blocked by Ralph Neely.

Then the second half began.

For Dallas, it took a long time to close in on the Packers—but finally did when, in the waning minutes of the third quarter Villanueva booted another field goal. This one, from the 32, narrowed things to 21-20. Prior to his kick, Green Bay had gotten down to the Dallas 23, where Pitts fumbled. Dallas had, in return, moved to the Packer 25, where they were held and set up the FG.

But with the Cowboys threatening to capture the lead, Green Bay again took charge—and fast. Anderson's 19-yard kickoff return gave the Packers the ball on their 26. First Starr passed to Dale for 43 yards. Then Taylor got 9 on 2 plays, 4 on a run, and 5 on a pass—and when Dallas was penalized 5 for delay of game it was first down on the 17. Pitts got another yard, and Starr then pitched to Boyd Dowler for the score. Six plays, 74 yards. And 28-20 on Chandler's PAT. One play later, the third quarter ended.

Midway through the final period, the Packers boosted their advantage to 34-20. It started on the Dallas 48 after a fair catch on a punt. This was an inspirational Starr march. Three times he hit on crucial third-down passes. With third and 19 on the Packer 43, he hit Fleming for 24. With third and 12 on the Dallas 35, he hit Taylor for 16. And with third and 19 on the Dallas 28, he hit Max McGee for all the yards that were left.

McGee, one of the real old pros of the Packers, had replaced Dowler who had been flipped high in the air on his touchdown catch and badly shaken. Taylor was so incensed that he had to be tugged off the field by Starr so as to avoid a fight—and undoubted banishment.

But with a 34-20 score and a chance to make it 35 and virtually out of Dallas' reach, Chandler missed the placement and the Cowboys still had a chance. (Ironically, before the game Chandler—having a poor kicking year—allowed that "five extra points will be just fine" as far as he was concerned, even if he didn't get a single field goal; and had he gotten his 5, the game would have been as good as over. In the last 2 games between the 2 teams, won by Dallas 21-12 and 21-3, Chandler had kicked 5 field goals but the Packers had scored nary a touchdown.)

160

When Dallas scored only once, Green Bay had its victory and a Super Bowl date with Kansas City of the American Football League, which got by Buffalo in its playoff 31-7.

This was the Packers' tenth National Football League title. For each man, it was worth about $8,500.

It was a particularly noteworthy championship win for Starr, who as the Packers' "gentleman" quarterback now has guided 4 NFL titleholders (1961, 1962, 1965, 1966), to match Sid Luckman's record of 1940, 1941, 1943, 1946 for the Chicago Bears. Starr completed 19 of 28 throws (67 percent) for 304 yards and 4 touchdowns, despite a Dallas rush that threw him for losses 5 times.

He was a master play-mixer as illustrated by his 4 touchdown strikes. He passed to Pitts for a 17-yard TD with second and 7, to Dale for 51 yards on first and 10, to Dowler for 16 yards on second and 9, and to McGee for 28 yards on third and 19.

As to the handful of times he was thrown trying to get the ball away, Starr observed, "When you play against a team like theirs and throw as much as we did today, you've got to expect to get caught once in a while—and I must point out, a number of times I almost got away. I thought the pass protection was outstanding. But, of course, it's been that way all year."

His opposite number, Meredith, had a good afternoon, hitting on 15 of 31 and gaining 238 yards, but his one touchdown toss was offset by the costly interception at the end. That the Packers double-teamed Bob Hayes deep obviously hampered the Cowboy aerial arm; the "world's fastest human" caught only 1 of the 4 throws that came his way—and for but a scant yard at that. Adderley, Willie Wood, and Bob Jeter shared the duties of covering him.

In the gloomy Dallas dressing room after the game, Meredith repeatedly was asked about his last play by the horde of reporters. "I thought it was the best play we had available at that point; I chose it mainly because you have the option of both running or throwing off it. It's a fake run and rollout to the weak side, and the weak-side linebacker will come up on the play and give us a chance to get outside him—but Robinson made a real strong move to the outside and took away our option. It was fourth down and

I had one receiver in the end zone, and I had to put the ball up there." For the interception.

Two of the preceding plays in that final series also drew comment. Meredith particularly lamented the illegal-motion penalty back to the 6, noting that otherwise the Cowboys would have had "a couple of plays to get in from a yard or so out . . . and the difference between one and six yards when you're at the Packer goal is enormous." And Reeves insisted on taking the blame for missing a sure TD pass on the following play: "The pass was good—I just dropped it. I was trying to run with it before I got it."

The two coaches' observations were what might have been expected of a disconsolate loser and a proud winner: Landry—"We had our chances and we muffed them. It's a bad way to lose . . . but Green Bay is a real good team and it's no embarrassment to lose to them." Lombardi—"They say we don't have offense—but we've got it when we need it! We didn't readjust in the second half, all we did was to get tougher and more aggressive. My heart's coming right out of my shirt . . ."

The Scoring:

Green Bay	14	7	7	6	—	34
Dallas	14	3	3	7	—	27

GB—Pitts 17, Starr pass (Chandler kick)
GB—Grabowski 18, fumble return (Chandler kick)
Dal.—Reeves 3, run (Villaneuva kick)
Dal.—Perkins 23, run (Villaneuva kick)
GB—Dale 51, Starr pass (Chandler kick)
Dal.—FG Villaneuva 11
Dal.—FG Villaneuva 32
GB—Dowler 16, Starr pass (Chandler kick)
GB—McGee 23, Starr pass (Chandler kick blocked)
Dal.—Clarke 68, Meredith pass (Villaneuva kick)

The Statistics:

	GB	Dal.
First downs	19	23
Yardage rushing	102	187
Yardage passing	304	238
Passing	19-28	15-31
Own passes intercepted	0	1
Penalties	23	29
Fumbles lost	1	1
Offensive plays	58	73

Individual Statistics:

Rushing

Green Bay—Pitts 12 attempts for 66 yards, Taylor 10 for 37, Starr 2 for minus 1.

Dallas—Perkins 17 attempts for 108 yards, Reeves 17 for 47, Meredith 4 for 22, Norman 2 for 10.

Passing

Green Bay—Starr attempts 28, completed 19 for 304 yards.

Dallas—Meredith attempts 31, completed 15 for 238 yards (1 interception).

Pass Receiving

Green Bay—Dale 5 receptions for 128 yards, Taylor 5 for 23, Fleming 3 for 50, Dowler 3 for 49, McGee 1 for 28, Pitts 1 for 17, Long 1 for 9.

Dallas—Reeves 4 receptions for 77 yards, Norman 4 for 30, Clarke 3 for 102, Gent 3 for 28, Hayes 1 for 1.

163

XVII

GREEN BAY PACKERS VS. BALTIMORE COLTS
(Game played December 26, 1965)

GREEN BAY, WIS. (Dec. 27, 1965)—In the encroaching dusk of Lambeau Field on a frigid December afternoon, the Green Bay Packers and Baltimore Colts struggled yesterday for nearly 3 hours of tension-fraught football before deciding who would rule the West.

And once more, the Packers reign supreme as Western Conference champions of the National Football League, victors over the Colts by 13-10. No NFL football game has ever lasted longer, not even the epic "sudden death" battle of 1958 when these same Colts defeated the New York Giants 23-17.

The Packers rule because of a 25-yard field goal by Don Chandler after 13 minutes and 39 seconds of sudden death—his second dramatic place-kick of the game. Chandler had had to boot an equally crucial field goal with less than 2 minutes of regulation time remaining in order to force the game into overtime. That kick was from the 22. Had he missed his earlier attempt, with just 1:58 to go in the fourth quarter, Baltimore would almost certainly have won a 10-7 upset—and it would have been a magnificent win for the gallant Colts, who on this long afternoon were without not just one but both of their regular quarterbacks.

Neither the nonpareil Johnny Unitas (with Alan Ameche, the hero of that memorable 1958 overtime) nor understudy Gary Cuozzo was even suited up yesterday, leaving the critical quarterbacking role to running back Tom Matte. And Matte almost pulled it off.

But the Packers, ever a defeat-resisting football team in the big game under Vince Lombardi, rallied themselves in the waning minutes of the final period and drove relentlessly to where Chandler could get a shot at victory—and a chance that they and the 50,484 chilled but enthralled spectators knew would never come again. But Chandler sped the ball off Bart Starr's fingertips through the uprights 22 yards away, and the Packers had their tie and were still alive. Nearly a full quarter of football later they were winners.

They were winners—and champions of the West—with their own great quarterback, Starr, on the sidelines (except for a handful of seconds). Starr had been badly racked up trying to wipe out blockers on a pass interception 21 seconds after the game began, returning to the field only to assist on place-kicks. In his place the Packers called on veteran backup quarterback Zeke Bratkowski—and like the unheralded Matte, he did an inspired job. Unlike his Colt counterpart, however, he won.

Whether Starr's tape-swathed ribs will be healed for next Sunday's NFL Championship game with the Cleveland Browns—also at Lambeau Field—was uncertain. Uncertain, too, was the condition of battered Paul Hornung, who took a punishing from the rugged Baltimore defense. "I can't get dressed," groaned Hornung as he sat wearily in the dressing room after the game with aching ribs, knee, and wrist—and he spoke and breathed with difficulty. Also nursing injuries were end Boyd Dowler, tight end Bill Anderson, and tackles Ron Kostelnik and Henry Jordan. Said defensive back Herb Adderley, "This was the roughest game I've ever been in!"

Before the Packers made their clutch drive from their own 20 to end the sudden-death period (a 9-play assault leading to Chandler's kick), the game had been one of repeated frustrations for Packer fans—starting on the first play of the game. On that play, Starr fired a pass to Anderson, who briefly held possession but then dropped the ball as he was belted hard by Colt defender Lenny Lyles. Don Shinnick scooped up the ball from the dazed Anderson and sprinted some 25 yards into the end zone. The scoreboard clock showed 21 seconds, the board 7-0.

That would have been bad enough from a Packer standpoint, but what really hurt was that Starr had to be heldped off the field by teammates after having been flattened trying to take out some of Shinnick's interference.

Bratkowski moved the Packers well the next 2 times they got the ball, but a midfield fumble stopped one march, and their next surge resulted in a missed field goal when they disdained crowd pleas to "go for it" with fourth and a foot on the 40.

Then in the second quarter, Baltimore got its running game working. They put together a series of rushes that moved the ball from its own 25 to the Green Bay 7-yard line (all but one play on the ground as Jerry Hill, Lenny Moore, and Matte did the damage) before being stymied by the Bay defense. Lou Michaels booted the ball home from the 15, and the Colts' lead was increased to 10-0. Nine and a half minutes had elapsed in the period.

When a pass interference call gave the Packers the ball deep in Baltimore territory on the 9, the green-and-gold squad had its first real opportunity of the game with less than 4 minutes remaining before half time. And the Packers thrust deeper immediately as Bratkowski hit Anderson at the 2.

But Baltimore stiffened. Jim Taylor could get nothing. Hornung lost a couple of feet on his try. And on fourth down Taylor, for a split second, seemed to have a gaping hole—only to have Michaels and Ordell Brasse hit him inches short of the goal line. It was a great stand.

But the Packers didn't fizzle their next chance. It came soon after the second half began, when a high snap from center forced kicker Tom Gilburg to leap frantically for the ball. Too late to punt it away, he had to run, was swarmed by rushing Packer linemen, and thus turned over possession to Green Bay on the Colt 35.

Two plays later Green Bay was on the 1 as fleet Carroll Dale was tripped but nevertheless managed to latch onto the ball for a spectacular catch. Two plays later "goal line-smelling" Hornung was in there. It had taken 5:05 in the half to narrow the gap to 10-7 after Chandler's PAT.

Down now by only a slim 3 points, the Packers began taking charge of the play—but twice were thwarted by pass interceptions. Bob Boyd got one of them, Jerry Logan the other. That second interception was particularly damaging, since the Packers were in excellent field-goal position on the 20.

Finally, with 9:03 left, Green Bay took over on its 28—obviously in desperate need of a long drive . . . and points. Time now began "hurting."

Dowler took a big pass for 11 to the 39; 3 more plays advanced the ball to the 50. Then came a game-swinging play—and lucky call. Bratkowski dropped back to pass and was overwhelmed by Colt defenders. Seemingly, the Packers would have possession on their 42 due to the loss. But instead, Billy Ray Smith was nailed for unnecessary roughness, and it was Green Bay's ball on the Colt 43—and another first down. Ray fumed—"That call cost us the ball game; it was a lousy call!"

Now fired up, the Packers took 3 plays to get to the 32—and after an incomplete pass, Anderson hauled one in on the 20. Things began looking grim for the sagging Colts.

But when Tom Moore and Taylor got 5 and Moore dropped a third-down pass with only 2:02 remaining in the game, there was only one thing Green Bay could do: Go for the tie.

They got their tie. Chandler trotted onto the field along with Starr, the aching but nerveless Bart positioned the ball perfectly, and Don sailed it between the sticks. Ten-all with 1:58 left.

"Between the posts" is not the way the glum Colts saw the kick soar, however. They insisted that the officials blew the call, maintaining that the ball was wide of the uprights. "It was wide by three feet" is the way a bitter Michaels put it; and "If that kick was good, I'll eat the football" was defensive end Fred Miller's assessment—among the more printable comments. The kick and 3 points obviously stood, however.

When the Packers won the toss, the sudden death began auspiciously for them—but only until Baltimore kicked off. Green Bay ran the ball out only to its 22 and could advance it no farther than the 24 before having to yield possession.

On the punt, Baltimore took over on its own 41 for good field position—so vital in overtime—but was unable to move the ball and had to kick it back to the Packers. Again, though, Green Bay could do nothing, and 3 plays forced another punt from the same spot it took over—its 21. This time Baltimore gave the shivering crowd a scare. Starting out on its 41 again, Matte drove the Colts to the Packer 37 (mostly on his own rollouts) before stalling.

Michaels had to drop back to the 47 for the attempted field goal—long, but nevertheless within his range; but the center Buzz Nutter's snap was a mite low, and the kick flew both wide and short and gave possession to the Packers on their 20. With 7:06 on the clock and the stadium lights necessary in the gloom.

168

By now Hornung was out with his accumulated injuries, and Elijah Pitts was in the backfield. And Pitts started things off with a sweep for 4. Bratkowski immediately fired to Anderson—having a great day—for a big 18 up to the 42. Green Bay emphatically was making its move. Two plays off the tackles by Pitts and Taylor gobbled up another 11 yards, and it was first down on the Colt 47. And when Taylor plunged for 3 and Dale made another clutch catch (this one a leaping snatch just prior to falling out of bounds), the Packers had 18 more on the 26.

Now Green Bay was in great field-goal range—and not about to mess things up by passing, running wide, or fumbling. They called for 3 shots at the center of the line by Taylor and Pitts. The three gained 8 helpful yards, making it just that much closer for the kick everyone in the stadium knew was going to come.

With the ball on the 18 and in the center of the field, rookie center Bill Curry hovered over the ball while Starr knelt to receive it on the 25. Everyone tensed, Packer cornerback Herb Adderley being so wrought up that he couldn't watch: "I just kept my head down and listened on the radio to what was happening."

The snap was true, the holding was sure, the kick was perfect. Thirteen minutes and 39 seconds of sudden death capping 60 minutes of regulation football was over. In the stands the 50,000 fans whooped and jumped—or stood numb after the almost unbearable tension. On the field, Colts sagged and trudged off to their dressing room . . . while jubilant, exulting Packers leaped about, clutched each other, and went emotionally limp. Said Dowler, "I've never been in a game so emotionally trying." Said Jordan, "This was the toughest game I've ever been in." Or Adderley, "This was the roughest game I've ever been in." Their sentiments expressed the way everybody felt.

The victory was perhaps especially precious to 2 men—34-year-old quarterback Zeke Bratkowski and 31-year-old Don Chandler. "We must have been the two most excited old men in the country today," observed Chandler. And Bratkowski glowed as he said "This is my tenth year in pro ball, but I've never been with a winner before." As a reserve and a castoff, winning was particularly sweet to them. Both had made notable contributions to that win, Zeke in hitting 22 of 39 passes for 248 yards and Don with his deadly place-kicking.

Another castoff who had a big day was Bill Anderson, the chief Packer passing target with 8 catches for 78 yards—and this despite being so groggy he could not recall game details. Baltimore Coach Don Shula lauded him for "beating our zone defense with hook-in patterns—and when we blitzed, Bratkowski hit him with the quick pop-pass." The former Washington Redskins tight end had come out of retirement this season.

Relaxing in the dressing room afterward, Packer defensive end Willie Davis explained a line adjustment that was perhaps decisive in stopping Baltimore during its major thrust in overtime, keeping it from a close-range field-goal try. Matte had ripped off 22 yards in 3 straight carries to move the Colts to the Packer 37—obviously mounting a dangerous threat. But at this point, old pro Davis took it upon himself to change the defense. "What I did was play head-on against the tackle and let Ray Nitschke take the outside. We were able to stack up those running plays after that." The effectiveness of the move is apparent from the fact that after Matte's 3 early gains of 9, 5, and 8 to the 37, the next 2 plays were for losses of 1 and 2 to force Michaels to drop back to the 47 for his place-kick.

Lombardi was visibly proud of his charges, noting that the team "was superb in adverse conditions—we gave a TD away early in the game and still stayed right in there. And those Colts did a great job without the horses; you've got to give Shula credit."

As Shula acknowledged, "You don't belong in this league if you play a team three times and can't even beat them once"—even though this third time was without a real quarterback. The Packers had scored 20-17 and 42-27 wins earlier in the campaign.

Without a "thrower," the Colts could not use their usual passing formula, and Matte (a handoff quarterback in college converted to a running back at Baltimore) put the ball in the air only 12 times. He completed 5 for just 40 yards. He ran with the ball more often, carrying 17 times and gaining 57 yards—thereby matching Hill's ball-toting performance.

Top ground-gainer was the Packers' line-busting fullback Taylor, with 23 hits for 61 yards. Hornung got 33 in 10 tries before going out with his injuries.

170

Green Bay's win settled the tie for Western division laurels with identical 10-3-1 records—and set up what could be a tremendous playoff game a week hence with Cleveland's 11-3 Eastern Conference kings.

And that game figured to be a toss-up, with the now-battered Packers facing a formidable Cleveland team led by the great Jim Brown, who this year has gained an awesome 1,544 yards in 289 carries and scored 21 touchdowns.

But it is yesterday's game that the pro football world is still marveling about—and the way it capped a remarkable Western Division season. A fantastic season. Green Bay had started out with 6 straight victories, but then slumped to lose 3 of the next 5. Baltimore had reeled off 8 consecutive wins after splitting its first 2 (its only loss being to the Packers, 20-17). But then a Detroit tie made it:

	W	L	T	Pct.
Baltimore	9	1	1	.900
Green Bay	8	3	0	.727

The Colts seemingly were home free. But then things began to happen around the league. The Chicago Bears clawed out a 10-0 upset of the Colts—an incredible shutout for Unitas—and when the Packers shaded Minnesota 24-19 in a last-minute sizzler, suddenly it was a race again. And when "Golden Boy" Paul Hornung went on a spectacular 5-touchdown spree as the Packers and Colts clashed in Baltimore (Green Bay winning 42-27), the standings looked like this:

	W	L	T	Pct.
Green Bay	10	3	0	.769
Baltimore	9	3	1	.750

One weekend remained. Incredibly, that last weekend produced the bizarre results necessary for a championship tie: A hairy 20-17 Baltimore win over the Los Angeles Rams and a 24-24 Packer tie with San Francisco's 49ers.

Baltimore had played its crucial contest on Saturday, giving it a

171

10-3-1 finish, and then had to sweat out Green Bay's climactic game the next day in Kezar Stadium. When Don Chandler kicked a 30-yard field goal with just 2 minutes to go, making it 24-17, the Packers seemingly had victory and the divisional championship assured. But John Brodie connected with rookie end Vern Burke on a 27-yard TD pass with just over a minute left, and the Packers were tied—and the television-watching Colts must have gone wild. Even so, Starr almost won the game on a long pass to Max McGee that was broken up by Kermit Alexander just as McGee's hands were reaching for the ball.

It was that kind of a season. No wonder yesterday's game was sudden death; it was the only appropriate way to end such a year.

The Scoring:

Baltimore	7	3	0	0	0	—	10
Green Bay	0	0	7	3	3	—	13

Ba.—Shinnick 25, fumble return (Michaels kick)
Ba.—FG Michaels 15
GB—Hornung 1, run (Chandler kick)
GB—FG Chandler 27
GB—FG Chandler 25

The Statistics:

	GB	Ba.
First downs	23	9
Rushing yardage	112	143
Passing yardage	250	32
Passes	41-23	5-12
Own passes intercepted	2	0
Punting	5-42	8-41
Fumbles lost	1	2
Penalties	4-40	3-59
Offensive plays (including times thrown)	81	60

Individual statistics:

Rushing

Green Bay—Taylor 23 attempts for 60 yards, Hornung 10 for 60, Pitts 3 for 14, Moore 3 for 5.

Baltimore—Hill 16 attempts for 57 yards, Matte 17 for 57, Moore 13 for 33, Lorick 1 for 1, Gilburg 1 for minus 5.

Passing

Green Bay—Bratkowski 22 attempts for 22 completions and 248 yards (2 intercepted), Starr 1 for 1 for 10 yds, Hornung 1 for 0.

Baltimore—Matte 12 attempts for 5 completions and 40 yards.

Receiving

Green Bay—Anderson 8 completions for 78 yards, Dowler 5 for 50, Hornung 4 for 42, Dale 3 for 63, Taylor 2 for 29, Moore 1 for minus 4.

Baltimore—Mackey 3 completions for 25 yards, Moore 2 for 15.

XVIII

GREEN BAY PACKERS VS. NEW YORK GIANTS
(Game played December 11, 1938)

POLO GROUNDS, NEW YORK CITY (Dec. 12, 1938)—In a game that was football at its primitive best, the New York Giants won the championship of the National Football League yesterday with a stirring come-from-behind 23-17 victory over the Green Bay Packers.

Punches were exchanged frequently as tempers flared in the 60 minutes of ultra-tension—and several players wound up being treated for injuries more serious than normally sustained in the bruising game of professional football. Both teams were obviously supremely fired up for the contest—and showed it in the sustained fierceness of their play.

It was a spectacular match-up of Eastern and Western divisional titleholders, begun in daylight before a playoff-record 48,120 spectators and ended under floodlights. The outcome illustrated the truth of the cliché, "The issue was in doubt until the final second." As the game ended, the Packers' strong-armed Arnold Herber was still throwing the ball, trying desperately to find a receiver in Giant territory.

This was a game of alternating momentum. New York had slammed into an early 9-0 advantage, capitalizing on back-to-back blocked punts and outplaying the Packers decisively. But Green Bay rallied in the second quarter and went into the half time locker room trailing by only 2, 16-14, and continued its resurgence by seizing a 1-point lead at the start of the second half. The Giants had the moxie to come back, however, and a concerted third-quarter surge wrested control again . . . this time for good.

The final quarter was scoreless but far from dull. Both teams had many scoring opportunities, albeit fruitless. And the game not only ended in anything-can-happen fashion on the field but with heated exchanges of views by the rival coaches. Typical of a losing mentor, Earl "Curly" Lambeau of the Packers was vehemently critical of officials' calls, while winning coach Steve Owen strongly upheld the officiating.

175

New York won with a solid show of force when it needed it. Statistics point to a marked Green Bay offensive superiority, some 362 yards to 216, but even rabid Packer backers acknowledged after the game that the Giants were probably the overall better team. It was essentially defense versus offense, and defense won out.

Perhaps the most significant aspect of the tilt is that Green Bay trotted onto the field without its most feared offensive weapon, breakaway pass-catcher Don Hutson. Hutson was sidelined with an injured knee (he had also missed the regular-season game that the New Yorkers won 15-3 in late November) and played only briefly. He tried his twisted knee for a few plays in the first half, and later gallantly limped in to try to set up a long-gainer pass play in the final seconds of the game. Without Hutson, the Wisconsin squad was hurting most severely.

With the nearly 50,000 spectators setting a playoff-game attendance record, the game produced gate receipts of $68,331.80—which put $504.45 into the pocket of each Giant and $368.84 into that of each Packer. That extra $135.61 the Giants earned came on a 23-yard aerial strike from Ed Danowski to Hank Soar midway through the third quarter, culminating a slashing 61-yard march that began immediately after the Packers had taken a 17-16 lead. Soar made a clutch catch in the midst of Packer defenders and busted over the goal line, with Clarke Hinkle vainly trying to stop him.

Prior to that clinching tally, the Giants had scored in the first period on a 14-yard field goal by Ward Cuff and a 6-yard plunge by Tuffy Leemans, and again in the second quarter on a 21-yard pass from Danowski to Feets Barnard. Cuff got the 2 successful placements.

Green Bay got its points on 2 second-quarter touchdowns and a 15-yard third-quarter field goal. Carl Mulleneaux scored first on a booming 40-yard pass from Herber, and Hinkle plunged a yard for the other 6-pointer. The 2 extra-point kicks and field goal were all booted by Tiny Engebretsen.

The Giants generally appeared to be in much better condition than the Packers, who had been idle since November 20 waiting for the Eastern division race to be decided. New York, however,

176

incurred the most crippling injuries. Although Packers repeatedly found themselves sprawled on the ground with hurts of one kind or another, they rarely were out of action for long. Not so with several Giants. Johnny Dell Isola wound up in St. Elizabeth's Hospital with a spinal concussion that was just short of being a fractured vertebra. Ward Cuff suffered a possible fracture of the sternum. Leland Schaffer came up with a badly sprained ankle that bordered on a break. And Mel Hein was kicked in the cheekbone at the end of the second quarter, suffering a concussion of the brain that left him temporarily bereft of memory—although he came to in the final quarter and finished out the game.

The Giant backfield was highly effective, with Soar, Leemans, and Danowski benefiting from some devastating blocking by the rugged Cuff. Up front the forward wall proved to be a game-long hard-to-budge unit from tackle to tackle, while ends Jim Poole and Jim Lee Howell constantly harassed Packer backs as they slashed in from the flanks. Danowski set up gains of 78 yards in completing 7 of 11 passes; Leemans whacked out 67 yards as a triple threat via running, receiving, and throwing 1 completion; and Soar amassed a fancy 106 yards both running and receiving.

Green Bay, of course, with its long-range overhead threat, had a handful of players with impressive yardage. Foremost were Herber and Cecil Isbell, primarily because of their passing. Herber accounted for 144 yards in all, 122 of them through the air by connecting on 5 of 14 tosses; while Isbell contributed 133 through the varied combination of passing, running, and receiving. And then there was the hard-hammering Hinkle, punching out 59 yards on sweeps or dives into the line—and ends Wayland Becker and Lee Mulleneaux, each with 2 receptions totaling 78 and 64 yards to help offset the absence of the dazzling Hutson. Press-box consensus held that the outstanding lineman on the field was Earl "Bud" Svendsen of the visitors. He was tremendous in the middle of the line.

An erratic bounce of Danowski's second punt of the game led to the first points of the game early in the contest. The ball was downed by Cuff deep in Packer territory on the 12-yard line. Two plays by Isbell got nowhere, and Hinkle went back to the goal line to punt on third down.

The kick went nowhere either as Howell crashed through to block it and Schaffer gathered it in for possession on the Packer 7. Becker and Russ Letlow piled up Soar for no gain, and then Bull Karcis met even more defenders as Mulleneaux, Hinkle, and Becker stopped him with a scant yard. And when Cuff stumbled going after Danowski's pass, it was fourth down and the ball still 6 yards away from a score. The Packers couldn't stop the next play, however, as Danowski set up on the 14 and Cuff booted a perfect field goal: 3-0, Giants.

A blocked punt set up the next score as well. Hinkle ran the kickoff back to his 22 and things started auspiciously for the Packers, as Isbell went wide to his left for 4, and the Giants drew an off-side penalty on the next play to make it second-and-1. But Hein and Cuff stopped Isbell cold at right tackle; and when Hinkle reversed to his left on third down, Howell and Poole collaborated to hurl him back for a 4-yard loss. The Packers had to kick again.

This time Isbell drew the assignment—and he met the same fate that befell Hinkle just a few minutes earlier. Poole came charging through to block it and Howell recovered on the 28.

But New York wasn't to be content with 3 points on this opportunity; it went all the way. And it went all the way in just 4 crackling plays. First Danowski pitched to Leemans for 5; next Tuffy sliced off right tackle for 4; and then the durable Leemans took it again to the left for 13 big ones down to the 6.

And Leemans didn't let up. He took the ball on his fourth try, slammed into the left-tackle slot, and simply cannonaded off Packer defenders to crunch into the end zone to cap a pulverizing drive. John Gildea's attempted PAT sailed wide of the posts, but it was a quick 9-0 lead for New York and the crowd began envisioning a romp.

Lambeau didn't see it that way, however. He immediately pulled 10 of his 11 first string players off the field, leaving in only Charles "Buckets" Goldenberg. While Green Bay took over in excellent field position on its 45 after an out-of-bounds kickoff, it again went nowhere and punted just as the first quarter ended.

It stopped New York this time, but the Giants shoved Green Bay back to its 8 on the next series. Herber got off a tremendous kick from the end zone, and Leemans ran it back 19 yards to the Packer 41 putting the Giants in great position again.

Two plays later, though, Hank Bruder deflected Leemans' pass to Engebretsen for an interception on the Packer 49. Hutson immediately decoyed, and the ruse helped Eddie Jankowski bull for a dozen to the New York 39. Andy Uram lost a yard, then couldn't hang onto a Herber pass. Then Herber hurled a long bomb that Mulleneaux got under at the 3 (after evading 3 Giants) and plucked in, scoring in a stride. When Engebretsen booted the ball for the extra point, it was a 9-7 ball game.

It didn't take long for the Giants to retaliate. After they had punted out of bounds on the Packer 23 soon after the kickoff, they gave up a 24-yard Herber-to-Uram pass to midfield but then Hein pounced on a first-down fumble by Jankowski on the 50. Three straight rushes by Leemans, and it was a Giant first down on the 40. Hinkle and Svendsen threw Len Barnum back 2 yards. Then on the next play Leemans flipped to Barnum, who fumbled when hit by Hinkle, but luckily the ball rolled out of bounds for New York possession on the 22. Another first down. Next it was Barnum's shot at the line, but he got a scant yard off right tackle. Danowski went to the air, and hit Barnard at the 2. Barnard hooked it in over Uram's shoulder, and New York had 6 more points. Cuff's placement boosted things to 16-7.

But Green Bay scored even more rapidly than the Giants when play resumed. A reverse lost 3 yards, and then came a bomb. Taking the ball on a direct snap from center, Isbell charged for the line but at the last moment leaped high and fired a pass to Becker. The lanky end pulled it in on the run and went sprinting into the clear along the sidelines on what seemed like a certain TD scamper. But Soar gave chase and finally overtook him on the Giant 17 to end a spectacular 66-yard play. It was only a temporary save, however. Isbell stumbled through right tackle on a spinner for 8, and then, with the ball on the 9-yard line, the calls went like this:

Hinkle—center for 1.
Hinkle—right guard for 3.

Hinkle—right guard for 3.
Hinkle—center for 1.
Hinkle—left tackle for 1 and the TD.

Engebretsen booted the placement, it was 16-14, and 4 plays later the half ended.

Nine plays after the second-half kickoff, Green Bay's surging Packers had scored again. Laws ran Cuff's kick a flashy 29 yards back to his 32 to start things off. And on the first play from scrimmage, the Giants not only gave up 4 yards to Laws but lost Dell Isola with a severe injury. Hinkle got a couple, and then it was Bobby Monnett's turn to cut loose. Behind the savage blocking of Champ Seibold and Svendsen, he turned the right end and scooted for 33 yards to the Giant 29 before Howell caught him. Hinkle then bumped past Cuff for 5, and belted Ward with a block to spring Laws for 10 more on the next play. Again Hinkle hammered through for 5, this time shaking off the grasp of 2 men. But Monnett, trying right end on the next play, ran into Cuff for no gain. And when Laws got only 3 off left end, the Packers decided to settle for a field goal. They got it, Laws holding on the 15 and Engebretsen drilling it home. That gave the Packers the lead for the first time, 17-16, and they also had the momentum.

But the Packers also had to kick off, and not until the Giants had marched all the way to and into the Green Bay end zone did they relinquish the ball—and by then they had scored and regained the lead.

Howell started them off by returning a low kick a dozen yards to his 39. Green Bay ganged up on Soar on the first scrimmage play, but then he shot around left end past midfield to the Green Bay 48 and a first down. Again Soar took it, this time ramming off tackle for 8. Then Green Bay stiffened. Milt Gantenbein forced Soar into Engebretsen's arms for a 2-yard loss, and when Danowski's pass to Howell got 3 it was a delicate fourth-and-1 situation. Soar banged left guard and got it. First down on the 38. And New York continued to make the most of Soar's talent and stamina: A 3-yard buck, an incomplete pass, then an up-the-middle reception by him for 9 yards to the 26. And after he picked up 3 off right tackle, it was Soar again for the payoff as he snatched Danowski's pass out of a cluster of Packers for 23 yards and the TD. Cuff's PAT made it 23-17 and the end of scoring, though not of excitement.

That scoring drive was a tremendous testimonial to Soar. Incredibly, he handled the ball on 10 of the 11 plays and gained 58 of the 61 yards in the march: 7 rushes, a pass, and 2 receptions!

Green Bay advanced 2 first downs to the New York 38 after the ensuing kickoff (the big play was a 22-yard pass gain by Isbell), but Danowski's pass interception on the 30 ended that threat.

Again Green Bay picked up a pair of first downs after the Giants' subsequent punt, but the attack stalled on the New York 45, and Herber had to punt. Becker downed the ball on the Giant 2-yard line, and Danowski's reply boot carried out only to his 35 to give the Packers an excellent opportunity. But 2 long TD passes were broken up by Cuff, Danowski, and Leemans. Then Becker fumbled as he was hit after a 12-yard first-down gain to the Giant 22. Another chance gone.

Soon after came a play that Lambeau fumed about. With the ball on the Packer 43, Herber pitched to Gantenbein for 18 and a first down—but the latter was ruled an ineligible receiver and the play was nullified. New York declined the penalty and took possession of the ball on the 43. Lambeau angrily charged that head linesman Larry Conover blew the call. "How he arrived at such a conclusion is beyond me, because Bernie Scherer, our other end, was at least a yard behind the line of scrimmage. Instead of our being in possession of the ball in Giant territory, New York took it over in our zone. The movies will prove that I'm right about this." As the volatile Packer coach acknowledged, "There is nothing that can be done about it now, but it just isn't fair for us to lose a game on account of incompetent officiating. That's my sincere opinion." Lambeau also castigated Conover for an earlier decision: "He was wrong, definitely, in the second period when he ruled Tuffy Leemans' pass to Len Barnum complete. Moving pictures of the play will prove that Barnum fumbled immediately, the ball going out of bounds, and that the receiver had not held it long enough to establish possession. Since that play led to a Giant touchdown, Conover's decision hurt us plenty."

While Conover could not be reached after the game, Steve Owen could—and he defended the ruling on the ineligible receiver: "Why, Gantenbein and Scherer were playing side by side on the line at the time; and it's to Conover's credit that he called the play as he saw it."

Fired up over the play, New York sought to pick up insurance points—and on the first try at scrimmage the irate Packers swarmed on Leemans so vigorously that they were assessed a 15-yard penalty for unnecessary roughness. Even with that help, however, the Giants could not advance deeper than the 28 and settled for a field-goal try from the 36 by Cuff that sailed wide.

A bullet pass to Scherer quickly got the Packers out to their 39; they punched to another on the Giant 46, but then the attack stalled as Herber's fourth-down boomer soared too long.

The Giants got 1 first down, then had to punt.

Taking over on their 20, the Packers still tried. Herber had to run in desperation as receivers were covered, and grabbed 16 yards. Then he lofted the ball to Mulleneaux, who in turn lateraled to the limping Hutson for a 24-yard gain to the New York 40. But under a fierce Giant rush on the last play of the game, Herber could only barely get the ball away and it fell harmlessly to the turf.

The Scoring:

Green Bay	0	14	3	0	—	17
New York	9	7	7	0	—	23

NY—FG Cuff 14
NY—Leemans 6, run
GB—Mulleneaux, 40 Herber pass (Engebretson kick)
NY—Barnard 21, Danowski pass (Cuff kick)
GB—Hinkle 1, run (Engebretsen kick)
GB—FG Engebretsen 15
NY—Soar 23, Danowski pass (Cuff kick)

The Statistics:

	GB	NY
First downs	14	10
Rushing yardage	149	118
Passing yardage	213	98
Passes	8-19	8-15
Own passes intercepted	1	1
Fumbles lost	2	0
Penalties	20	10

Individual Statistics:

Rushing

Green Bay—Hinkle 17 attempts for 59 yards, Monnett 4 for 29, Herber 3 for 22, Isbell 11 for 20, Jankowski 2 for 13, Laws 3 for 10, Uram 2 for minus 1, P. Miller 1 for minus 3.

New York—Soar 21 attempts for 65 yards, Leemans 13 for 42, Barnum 3 for 8, Danowski 1 for 4, Karcis 3 for 3, Cuff 1 for minus 4.

Passing

Green Bay—Herber 14 attempts for 5 completions and 122 yards, Isbell 5 for 3 and 91 yards (1 interception).

New York—Danowski 11 attempts for 7 completions and 78 yards, Leemans 2 for 1 and 20 yards (1 interception), Barnum 1 for 0, Soar 1 for 0.

Receiving

Green Bay—Becker 2 completions for 78 yards, C. Mulleneaux 2 for 64, Uram 1 for 24, Isbell 1 for 22, Scherer 1 for 19, Gantenbein 1 for 6.

New York—Soar 3 completions for 41 yards, Howell 2 for 11, Barnard 1 for 21, Barnum 1 for 20, Leemans 1 for 5.

XIX

CHICAGO BEARS VS. SAN FRANCISCO 49ERS
(Game played December 12, 1965)

CHICAGO, ILL. (Dec. 13, 1965)—Ernie Nevers did it back in 1929. Dub Jones did it in 1951. And now a sensational rookie named Gale Sayers has done it too in this year of 1965. What these 3 men—and only these 3—have done is to score a remarkable 6 touchdowns in one football game. And in the most demanding of all football leagues, the NFL.

Sunday's spree by the amazing Sayers far outshone a tremendous team performance by his Chicago Bears in demolishing the San Francisco 49ers, 61-20, to keep themselves at least mathematically in the championship race. Two club records for regular-season play were set by the Bears yesterday—the 61 points and 9 touchdowns. And amazingly, back in the September opener, San Francisco had flattened the Bears, 52-24!

Oddly enough, the Bears also figured in both of the 2 previous 6-TD solo spectaculars. Nevers got his 6 on November 28, 1929, for the Cardinals, and Jones his 6 for Cleveland on November 25, 1951. Both times Chicago was the victim. For the awed crowd of 46,278 spectators, the turnabout was far more fun.

How did Sayers get those 6?

1. An 80-yard pass from Rudy Bukich.
2. A 21-yard run.
3. A 7-yard run.
4. A 50-yard run.
5. A 1-yard plunge.
6. An 85-yard punt return.

As the game ended, Sayers was on his way to a possible record-breaking seventh; he had plucked in a punt on his 19-yard line and sped back to midfield with it before being stopped on a near-breakaway runback.

The dazzling Kansas rookie obviously sped over a prodigious amount of yards during this day—and on a field made slick by occasional showers. How many did he gain?

134 yards on punt returns.
113 yards on 9 rushes.
89 yards on 2 pass catches.
That's 336 in all.

Incidentally, his 6 touchdowns boosted his season total to 21 and established a new National Football League record. Cleveland's Jimmy Brown had 20 going into his game with Los Angeles, but failed to get another score.

How did Papa Bear owner-coach George Halas feel about his rookie's dazzling day? "It was the greatest performance ever by one man on a football field; I never saw such a thing in my life!" Halas recalled that when Nevers had set his record the field was frozen ("you could spit and it would turn into an icicle before it hit the ground"), whereas yesterday's field was soft on top but firm underneath so that it provided reasonable footing. He cannily provided the Bears with slightly longer nylon cleats for the game, giving them just a smidgen more "bite" into the sod. The 71-year-old pro football patriarch admitted to keeping Sayers on the bench late in the game—despite constant chants from the stands to send him in—to avoid any possible injury, although he acknowledged that "I knew about the record and nobody was hungrier than I was for Gale to break it."

San Francisco coach Jack Christiansen left the premises quickly and quietly without making himself available for comment. His coaching aides and players, however, had plenty to say about yesterday's game—and most particularly about Sayers.

First, though the game itself. It was, of course, utterly sensational. One rather remarkable note must be injected, however. Incredibly, on this same day a thousand miles eastward in Baltimore's Memorial Stadium, Green Bay Packer "Golden Boy" Paul Hornung also was running wild. He scored 5 touchdowns (3 by running, 2 by passing for some 176 yards) to pace the Packers to a stunning 42-27 victory over the Colts and thereby move a half-game into the divisional lead with but one game remaining in the regular season. Had it not been for Sayers' phenomenal afternoon, the colorful Packer halfback would have been acclaimed from coast to coast for his brilliant clutch performance in a win-or-else situation. Sayers simply outstaged him.

Halas felt his squad seemed "a little flat" before the game and gave them a pep talk that apparently had an effect. The Bears hit hard both on attack and defense, and Sayers was sensational. Surprisingly, he was extremely effective in operating off the triple formation wherein 3 backs or wide receivers spread out on one side; that setup ordinarily is more oriented toward the pass than the run, but it also made the defense deploy wide and enabled a devastating runner such as young Sayers to break free repeatedly.

After just 2:27 had elapsed in the first quarter, Sayers sprinted 80 yards for a score with a pass, setting up his blocking superbly as he went. Before the quarter ended, burly Mike Ditka got beyond his man to race 29 yards for another score, capping an 81-yard drive. Roger Leclerc's place-kick after the second TD made it 13-0, a pass having failed on the first tally.

It stayed at 13-0 until late in the second period, when both teams scored 2 quick touchdowns in just 5 and a half minutes. San Francisco got the first when quarterback John Brodie capped a 10-play march of 78 yards by pitching to Dave Parks for the score—one of Parks' 9 catches for 129 yards. During the game Brodie hit on 19 of 37 tosses for 250 yards, the rest of the 49ers' aerial weaponry belonging to George Mira.

But Jon Arnett ran the kickoff back in spectacular style to set up the Bears immediately for a retaliatory TD; he would have gone all the way had not Jimmy Johnson fought off a blocker for a good 10 yards and then got free to nail Arnett on the 21 in a great show of individual defensive effort. The effort went for naught, however, when on the very next play Sayers burst free to score—this time leaping over Johnson a stride from the goal line to fly into the end zone. The time on Sayers' second of his historic 6 TDs was 10:10 elapsed in the period.

Then it was the 49ers' turn again, this time with John David Crow ripping in on a short 15-yard pass from Brodie after they had smashed back with the kickoff. And this TD was to produce history of a negative sort, for after it Tommy Davis missed the extra point—his first miss after a fantastic string of 234 consecutive conversions. Up to this point, he hadn't missed since entering the NFL 7 years ago!

Some felt the snap from center was low, others blamed the wet ball—but Davis himself in the locker room refused to alibi the miss: "The ball just slipped off to the right and that was that."

Now it was Chicago's turn. It didn't have much time left in the half but it had enough. A good runback, more crisply executed plays, and with 14:29 gone in the quarter Sayers was in the end zone with his third TD: 27-19 at the halfway mark. Still very much a ball game.

And Sayers started things off in the second half. With the ball on the 50, he burst clear of the immediate secondary and just kept running until he was in the end zone. The time was 3:50 elapsed. On this one, as on the others, the Bears delivered crushing blocks; Ditka and Johnny Morris bowled down close-up men on the right side, and Bob Wetoska and Ronnie Bull mowed down others barring the way. With this help, plus his own craft, Sayers had no problem.

Not until 13:49 remained in the period did the Bears score again—and, of course, it was Sayers. By now it was simply a question of what the final score would be—and how many points Sayers would get. A 1-yard plunge did it this time. A fumbled snap from the center messed up the PAT, but still it was 40-13 and a runaway.

San Francisco got on the boards first in the final quarter, Dave Kopay banging in for the final yard. It was a neat march by San Francisco, going 80 yards with 3 key passes figuring keenly—the first for 20 to Parks, the next for 37 to Dale Messer, and the third for 11 to Vern Burke. But the score was still doubled at 40-20.

An 8-yard pass from Bukich to rookie Jimmy Jones (who caught slings of 54 and 51 yards during the afternoon) accounted for the next Chicago touchdown—and then it was Sayers' turn again. This time he rambled 85 yards with a punt return (8:06 gone) for the record-tying TD No. 6.

Thereafter Arnett scored on a 2-yard plunge to make it 61 (after another Leclerc kick) and end things.

It had been a demoralizing day for the 49ers, who had come into the game leading the league in 13 statistical departments. Their supposedly robust rushing game managed only 58 yards, and while Brodie and relief man Mira did well in the air, it by no means could match the Bears' output. And neither team could truly claim the troublesome field to be a factor, inasmuch as there were only 3 fumbles and in no case did the ball go to the other team. Moreover, not once did the Bears crunch a 49er passer for a loss, which testifies to the solid forward wall of the West Coast 11. Nor, for that matter, did Chicago suffer a passing-attempt loss.

The fact that the combined teams gained a huge total of 864 yards is testimony to their ability to get over the semifrozen ground—mostly through the air (673 yards). The throwers and their receivers obviously knew how to get together on the slippery footing.

In the dressing rooms after the game, it was all Sayers. Nothing else mattered. And both teams concurred.

The losers were perhaps the more eloquent—and stunned. Among their observations: Assistant Coach Y. A. Tittle, himself one of pro ball's all-time best quarterbacks: "It was the most brilliant exhibition I've ever seen!" Defensive back Elbert Kimbrough: "He's out of sight!" Elaborated Kimbrough: "Sayers is the greatest—and that includes Jimmy Brown! He doesn't have Brown's power, but who needs power when you can run like that! He's always thinking ten yards ahead; his idea is that he wants to squeeze another ten yards out of the run and then another ten. And that high knee action makes it hard to bring him down—you can't lock both ankles (you hit him high and those knees keep pumping anyhow). A defensive player hates to commit himself against him because once you do that, he's off in another direction—but still you can't just set back for him because you know he'll go around you anyhow." Defensive back George Donnelly (who, incidentally, suffered a broken hand): "He looks no different than any other runner when he's coming at you, but when he gets there he's gone. You've simply got to contain him before he gets loose."

And Sayers' teammates, too, were unstinting in their praise. For instance: Bennie McRae: "He's unbelievable; what can you say about a guy like that!" Mike Rabold: "You know, he never says 'boo' . . . he's kind of at a disadvantage because he's a rookie—but as far as Jim [Cadile, another guard] and I are concerned, he's as seasoned as anybody who's been in the league six-seven years. He sets up our blocks for us . . . he stays right with us so when we make the block he knows he's going to take advantage of it (instead of going the other way) . . . and he has a great way of using his moves to set up the defensive halfbacks, making them commit themselves—and then he slaps one of us on the back and we take the guy out."

Sayers also acknowledged the blocking as being superb: "I had real good blocking on every play" and called his 80-yard pass run the biggest kick from the standpoint of bamboozling the traffic. However, when asked whether the day was his greatest thrill ever, he qualified his answer somewhat by noting that it was his biggest moment "in pro football." The 22-year-old phenomenon had once scored 4 TDs in a prep all-star game and, of course, had had a sensational college career.

After the game, the Bears did the only thing they could possibly have done: give him the game ball, complete with serenade.

Brilliant as Sayers' individual accomplishments were, it was also a great team effort—and an extremely important game for the Bears. Coupled with the Packers' upset of Baltimore, it made for a vigorous dogfight in the NFL's Western division. If the 49ers now can knock off Green Bay next weekend in San Francisco . . . and if Los Angeles can beat Baltimore next weekend in LA . . . and if the Bears can beat Minnesota here next weekend . . . *then* it could mean a divisional playoff with the Packers the day before Christmas.

But those are all *ifs*. One other dressing room observation has an "iffy" aspect to it, too, that merits pondering; mused Tittle after the game: "I wonder how many [touchdowns] that Sayers would have scored if we hadn't set our defense to stop him."

It was, surely, one of the great days.

190

CHICAGO BEARS VS. SAN FRANCISCO 49ers, 1965

The Scoring:

San Francisco	0	13	0	7	—	20
Chicago	13	14	13	21	—	61

Chi.—Sayers 80, Bukich pass (pass fails)
Chi.—Ditka 29, Bukich pass (Leclerc kick)
SF—Parks 9, Brodie pass (Davis kick)
Chi.—Sayers 21, run (Leclerc kick)
SF—Crow 15, Brodie pass (kick fails)
Chi.—Sayers 7, run (Leclerc kick)
Chi.—Sayers 50, run (Leclerc kick)
Chi.—Sayers 1, run (no kick, fumbled snap)
SF—Kopay 1, run (Davis kick)
Chi.—Jones 8, Bukich pass (Leclerc kick)
Chi.—Sayers 85, punt return (Leclerc kick)
Chi.—Arnett 2, run (Leclerc kick)

The Statistics:

	Chi.	SF
First downs	21	19
Rushing yardage	183	58
Passing yardage	401	272
Passes	17-33	23-44
Own passes intercepted	0	2
Punting	3-33	6-49
Fumbles lost	0	0
Penalties	6-30	2-14

XX

GREEN BAY PACKERS VS. CHICAGO BEARS
(Game played September 15, 1935)

GREEN BAY, WIS. (Sept. 16, 1935)—The names are Arnie Herber and Don Hutson, and the 14,000 people who were in City Stadium on Sunday won't soon forget them. And those fans who weren't there would do well to remember them, too—for Herber-to-Hutson could be something spectacular in football.

They teamed up yesterday on one stunning play to defeat the Chicago Bears, 7-0. Who was the more surprised—the Bears, Coach George Halas, or the spectators—would be hard to tell. And conceivably, even Coach Curly Lambeau and his Packers were almost as startled by the instant success of their well-planned, scintillating all-the-way strike.

The game began ordinarily enough. Chicago kicked off, Hank Bruder ran it back to his 17, and the ball game was under way. An ordinary start.

The next few seconds were extraordinary. Center Frank Butler snapped the ball back to Herber and the husky halfback faded back to his 4-yard line, pumping the ball toward the right as highly feared veteran Johnny Blood sped down the sidelines from his flanker spot on that side of the field. Blood raced at full speed toward the distant goal, luring Bear defensemen toward him in respect for his acknowledged skills. Only one other man headed upfield as the rest of the Packers pass-blocked to give the strong-armed Herber time to catapult the ball. That one man was Hutson, playing for the first time in Green Bay green-and-gold.

Hutson "went." He took off from his widespread left-end position, heading straight for the Bears' nearest defense man, right halfback Gene Ronzani—but then cut sharply toward the middle after giving him an outside fake that for a split second tipped Ronzani toward the sidelines. That was enough. With his first threat behind him, Hutson simply turned on the speed and angled for the goal line; he caught Herber's pass in full stride on the Chicago 45 and used his sprinter's speed to outrun Beattie

Feathers with astonishing ease. Feathers had been drawn over to cover Blood, and fast though he was—and a proven All-Pro—he just could not react quickly enough to catch the younger and faster rookie.

It was an 83-yard touchdown play, 50 yards of which involved Herber's perfectly thrown spiral while Blood was decoying beautifully and the unheralded Hutson was making his feint and then his goalward dash. The last 40-odd yards were a foot race, with Hutson an easy winner.

Bobby Monnett then came in to kick the extra point and Green Bay led, 7-0. There was no other score.

Hutson later explained that "on the first play the Bears converged on Johnny Blood, all but ignoring the pass. I lined up several yards wide because Curly [Lambeau] didn't want me boxed in by a big defense man I couldn't handle. I ran straight past Beattie Feathers, I believe, at midfield, and Herber's pass was perfect." Big tackle Cal Hubbard elaborated: "We figured they didn't have a very good book on Hutson . . . we decided we'd throw to him on the first play. We won the toss and elected to receive. We lined up in a spread . . . you know Arnie Herber could throw the ball a mile. Hutson faked to the outside, went behind their safety, took the pass, and went all the way."

Lambeau drew praise after the game for having conceived the play. Among the remarks: Guard Mike Michalske—"It was Lambeau's idea to move Don Hutson out on the flank; this is the first time any team has used or seen a flanker." Halfback Johnny Blood—"It's the first time a split end and flanker was used, and he scored a touchdown on the first play; that split end is Mr. Lambeau's invention."

Even one of the rival Chicago Bears chimed in with his view on the play—stellar halfback Johnny Sisk: "Johnny Blood was Green Bay's top receiver—then they double-crossed us on the first play and Hutson made it work." Among Sisk's other comments on Hutson were that he can "really turn it on . . . has a lot of changes of pace . . . can outmaneuver almost anybody and has speed . . . a rare football player . . . a once-in-a-lifetime guy."

Hutson has come to the Packers with impressive credentials: an All-American end at Alabama who scored 3 touchdowns in the

Crimson Tide's victory over Stanford in the 1935 Rose Bowl game—on breakaway passes. He'd gone to Alabama on a scholarship because of friends, and was at first more outstanding in track with such clockings as a 9.7 in the 100-yard dash and a 21.3 in the 220. But with Dixie Howel as a senior thrower, he became a "name" as a senior. In high school at Pine Bluff, Arkansas, he had hardly been distinguished.

He had been voted by the nation's football buffs to the College All-Star Game in Chicago's Soldier Field and hence had been late reporting to Green Bay. So he didn't figure in the opening National Football League game last week when the Packers excruciatingly lost to the Chicago Cardinals, 7-6. Milt Gantenbein and Al Rose were the ends then (and in that one, Monnett's crucial extra-point kick was wide).

When he did report to the Packers, his slight build was greeted with consternation: He packed only 177 pounds on a 6-1 frame. But he showed real class in practice, and so Lambeau and the whole Packer squad felt that they had something to spring on people—regardless of Green Bay's acid comments that "Curly made a boner" in signing a "skinny" end who couldn't possibly survive the punishing play of NFL football. Most especially against the Bears, who have long been noted for their vicious manhandling play. But Hutson didn't flinch at the criticism.

That he came to Green Bay at all was a matter of fate and 17 minutes. As a marked man on the Alabama team, Hutson had been well scouted. Among the scouts were Lambeau and John "Shipwreck" Kelly of the Brooklyn Dodgers. Both liked him. Lambeau mailed a contract to Hutson after the Rose Bowl game—in response to which Don twice wired Kelly (collect, of course) in Brooklyn to inform him of the Green Bay offer. But Kelly was vacationing in Florida and the telegrams didn't reach him immediately. When he got them, he chartered an airplane and flew to Alabama to talk to Hutson—too late, for Lambeau already had his signed contract in the mail. Kelly insisted that the Green Bay contract didn't count and offered Hutson several hundred dollars more to sign with Brooklyn—and so Hutson also signed that contract and mailed it in. NFL President Joe Carr got both documents in the mail on the same day. It was tricky. But since the Packer pact had been stamped at 8:30 on arrival and the Brooklyn one at 8:47, he honored Green Bay's contract. It had been sent special delivery.

So Hutson was signed at $175 a game. These days players are contracted for on a game-by-game basis. Some day they may be inked on a seasonal setup, but that is in the future. At any rate, the Packers did get Hutson—and he may turn out to be one of the great ones. Only time will tell. With a pass-oriented game such as Lambeau uses, he could wind up catching as many as 100 touchdown passes before he is through. Certainly, Sunday showed that his promise is considerable. Teammate Charles "Buckets" Goldenberg put it this way after the game: "I think it was a lucky break for Don as well as for the Packers to come here; if he had gone to Brooklyn he might not be in the league long . . . after all, Curly is the only coach getting much out of the pass—and we have a good team to give him support." Anyway, Hutson scored on that first burst Sunday—and he surely will be scoring again. And often. With Herber there to throw the ball long and Cecil Isbell in reserve to fling it almost as well, the Packers have a scoring threat par excellence—and if he has the stamina (and the luck to avoid crippling injuries), Hutson could go on to be legendary. He surely has the potential.

But back to the ball game.

The Packers zipped ahead 7-0 in the opening seconds and that is the way the game ended. But there was more to it than that. After injured Roger Grove came in to hold Monnett's place-kick for the seventh point, the Packers kicked off—and for a time neither team could effectively move the ball. But after several exchanges of punts, Joe Laws made a shifty 30-yard runback to the Bear 27, and Green Bay was threatening.

Bruder got 2 and then, after his pass to Al Rose was dropped, Monnett hit up center on a spinner for 7 to the 18 making the most of blocks by Butler and Tar Schwammel. But with fourth and a yard, Bill Karr and Gene Ronzani stopped Monnett cold and the attack was stalled.

Later on, Feathers' quick kick was run back 10 yards by Laws to the Chicago 45, and again the Packers seemed to be in position to move in—except that a 25-yard clipping penalty shoved them

196

back. Whereupon Bruder quick-kicked, Feathers taking the ball and slipping down on his 26.

Now it was Chicago's turn to advance. The Bears banged out a first down to the 37, then another when Ronzani picked up Keith Molesworth's fumble for a freak 10-yard gain to the 47. Stopped for no yardage on 2 plays, the Bears then drew a 5-yard penalty for too much time, and it appeared that their march would come to a halt. But Ronzani here drilled a pass to Molesworth on the left, and he scooted 40 yards to the Packer 18 before Monnett finally ran him out of bounds.

Here, though, the march did stop. Claude Perry and Michalske ganged up to stop Molesworth after a yard off right tackle, and Tar Schwammel yielded nothing around right end. When Ronzani lofted a pass to Ed Kawal in the end zone it was knocked away by Monnett and Earl "Bud" Svendsen, and Green Bay took over. The play ended the quarter.

On the first play after taking George Sauer's punt on its own 45, however, Chicago wasted no time in threatening again—and even more dangerously. The Bruin machine went into a pass formation and clicked on a 42-yard gain from Molesworth to Bill Pollock to the Packer 13, where Sauer made the tackle. Molesworth immediately got 5 around right end. But after Clarke Hinkle batted away Bob Dunlap's pass, a throw by Pollock was deflected by Bob O'Connor and Gantenbein wound up with an interception.

Green Bay then marched to the Chicago 30 before it, too, was halted by an interception—this one by Pollock, who lateraled to Molesworth for a return of a dozen yards to the Bear 33. That was the last excitement of the half.

The Packers came up with a couple of early threats in the second half. The first was on the initial exchange of punts, positioning the ball on the Green Bay 49. Monnett passed to Goldenberg for 15 to Chicago's 36. But 3 plays by Blood left the ball on the 33, and Schwammel dropped back for a field-goal try with Monnett holding on the 40—but Tar's kick just missed. Shortly afterward the stands were in an uproar as a fight broke out on the field, with Frank Butler and Bernie Masterson exchanging punches. Both were ejected.

When Chicago was forced to punt, Green Bay next took over on the 50, and 3 plays by Blood and Swede Johnston up the middle shoved the ball to the 41. That made it fourth and 1, and Lambeau ordered another field-goal try, this time with Blood holding on the 50—but again Schwammel's kick just slid wide of the uprights.

George Grosvenor then burst free on the Bears' first try from scrimmage, using Manders' blasting block to sweep around left end for 32 high-wheeling yards to the Packer 48. Then hulking Hubbard hurled Grosvenor 3 yards back, and soon afterward, the Chicagoans had to punt.

They had another opportunity just a couple of minutes later when Bruder's short punt went out of bounds on the Green Bay 43. Ronzani immediately cleared left end for 20 yards behind crushing blocks by Manders and Dunlap, and the Packers were in real trouble. They were in more trouble 2 plays later, as Grosvenor twice got 5 yards on the right side of the line. First down on the 13.

But here Green Bay held. Herman Schneideman held Grosvenor to a yard off right end as the third quarter ended, and when Hutson took out the interference on the next play Gantenbein slammed down Grosvenor for just another yard. Gantenbein was injured on the tackle, however, and had to be replaced by Bob Tenner.

That was the deepest the Bears could penetrate, Halas calling for 2 passes that failed—including a particularly intricate 1 on fourth down with Manders lateraling to Ronzani, whose pass to Bill Hewitt in the end zone went awry under a vigorous rush by Schneideman.

Chicago had only 2 more chances in Packer territory. One came when Manders recovered a fumble on the Bay 43. The other came with a short march to the 33 that started out well when Molesworth flipped to Ronzani for 6 to the 27 but ended with Perry and Lon Evans dropping George Corbett for a 5-yard loss on an attempted lateral and 2 passes falling incomplete.

Thereupon the Packers mustered one last threat themselves. When, late in the game, Blood took advantage of Bruder's solid blocking to run a punt back to his own 37 before Ookie Miller got him, the Bays made their move. Sauer started them off by breaking right tackle for 17 to the Chicago 46, and 2 plays later Blood passed to Tenner for 29 to the 19.

But here the Bears stiffened. An incomplete pass was followed by 2 line smashes for 7½ yards by Sauer and Hinkle, and Green Bay had to put the ball in the air—which resulted in Molesworth's interception of Blood's throw on the 9 to end it.

The Packers hurled the next 3 Bear plays back for a minus 5 yards. Blood ran Molesworth's punt back to the Bear 42, and 2 plays later Sauer lofted a long bomb to Blood that the irrepressible "Vagabond Halfback" snatched out of a pack of Bears down on the 5-yard line. But the gun had cracked as the play was run off, and there was no time left.

Sidelights:

Fans—most of them rabid Green Bay rooters—had ample opportunity to vocalize during the game for reasons other than the play on the field. In addition to the aforementioned fisticuffs between Butler and Masterson, who were ejected, there were several other exchanges of punches. In particular, there was a mix-it-up session between Blood and Joe Kopcha, also in the third period. And frequently the stands would point to one player or another with outcries of slugging, to no avail, as officials missed most such altercations.

Bear end Bill Hewitt drew his share of fans' attention—as usual—in the fourth quarter when on 2 successive plays he lined up fully 5 yards off side but was not penalized . . . and also when he got involved in a heated argument with referee Bobby Cahn over a fair-catch signal by Monnett during the third quarter, a dispute which—as usual—Cahn won. Hewitt did, however, save the Bears a 5-yard penalty in the same period when he alertly called time out just as Cahn seemed about to call an infraction on them for taking too much time in the huddle.

Bronko Nagurski was sorely missed by the Bears, both for his powerful running and his sledgehammer blocking. The injured fullback sat on the bench with his former Minnesota coach,

Clarence "Doc" Spears—now head man at the University of Wisconsin.

While the game-opening Herber-to-Hutson touchdown pass naturally was the single outstanding play of the contest, the steadfast play of Green Bay's burly linemen had knowledgeable fans applauding repeatedly. The interior linemen between the ends averaged 239 pounds: tackles Tar Schwammel at 230 and Cal Hubbard at 265, guards Walt Kiesling at 260 and "Iron Mike" Michalske at 210, and center Frank Butler at 230.

The Scoring:

Chicago	0	0	0	0	—	0
Green Bay	7	0	0	0	—	7

GB—Hutson 83, Herber pass (Monnett kick)

The Statistics:

	Chi.	GB
First downs	11	7
Rushing yardage	133	121
Passing yardage	96	183
Passes	5-26	7-17
Own passes intercepted	2	3
Fumbles lost	0	1
Penalties	30	40

Individual Statistics:

Rushing

Green Bay—Sauer 7 attempts for 37 yards, Hinkle 5 for 28, Blood 7 for 14, Herber 1 for 12, Johnston 3 for 9, Bruder 4 for 8, Monnett 3 for 7, Goldenberg 2 for 5, Laws 1 for 1.

Chicago—Grosvenor 9 attempts for 48 yards, Ronzani 12 for 44, Manders 9 for 28, Feathers 5 for 19, Molesworth 6 for 5, Corbett 1 for minus 5, Masterson 1 for minus 6.

Passing

Green Bay—Herber 6 attempts for 3 completions and 98 yards (1 interception), Blood 7 for 2 and 34 yards (2 interceptions), Monnett 3 for 1 and 15 yards, Sauer 1 for 1 and 36 yards.

Chicago—Molesworth 5 attempts for 3 completions and 55 yards, Ronzani 7 for 1 and 40 yards, Feathers 1 for 1 and 1 yard, Dunlap 5 for 0, Pollock 3 for 0 (1 interception), Corbett 2 for 0, Masterson 1 for 0, Manders 1 for 0 (1 interception), Crawford 1 for 0.

Receiving

Green Bay—Blood 2 completions for 45 yards, Hutson 1 for 83, Tenner 1 for 29, Goldenberg 1 for 15, Rose 1 for 6, Gantenbein 1 for 5.

Chicago—Pollock 1 completion for 42 yards, Molesworth 1 for 40, Johnsos 1 for 7, Ronzani 1 for 6, Hewitt 1 for 1.

XXI

GREEN BAY PACKERS VS. BELOIT FAIRIES
(Game played November 23, 1919)

BELOIT, WIS. (Nov. 24, 1919)—A single touchdown on Sunday decided the championship of Wisconsin professional football as the stalwart Beloit Amateur Athletic Club warriors thwarted the claim of Green Bay's Packers to that title by scoring a monumental 6-0 victory at Morse Field.

More properly, a single touchdown was ruled good by the officials but several were nullified—and the "real" score of the game will no doubt be argued forevermore.

The contest, played before a huge—and often unruly—crowd of more than 2,000 fans, was a fitting championship battle between these two fine groups of Midwestern athletes in moleskin. At no time during the game was the outcome certain.

But thrilling as the game itself was, the intensely vehement arguments between the wrathful gladiators and the officials—mostly involving the defeated Packers—will likely be remembered longest. Beloit Referee Baldy Zabell in particular was the focus of most Green Bay bitterness. Whereas the Beloit team and its gleeful followers were decidedly satisfied with the result, such was far from the case with the disgruntled visitors. To a man, the Packers angrily charged that they had been "robbed" of victory by home-town officiating—not to mention interference by the surging spectators.

Green Bay's Manager George Calhoun immediately issued a challenge for a rematch on December 7, to which Manager D. F. McCarthy of the AACs quickly agreed—although realizing that his Beloiters have nothing to gain and everything to lose by another game with the now-defeated Packers. The sum of $200 will be deposited in the Beloit State Bank, guaranteeing that the field will be kept free of spectators and that a fence will be placed around the gridiron 10 feet back of the sidelines. Efforts will also be made to obtain neutral officials, such as the famous Walter Eckersall of Chicago and other Western Conference referees. Both teams have also agreed to make deposits guaranteeing no "ringers" in their lineups. The Packers were also talking of organizing a special train to bring at least 500 fans from Green Bay to provide their own sideline support.

Only in the event of extremely inclement weather will the December game be called off. McCarthy indicated that should there be freezing rain or snow that weekend he may cancel the affair, inasmuch as 4 of his players are basketball men and he will not permit them to risk injury playing on an icy field.

Green Bay had been favored to win yesterday's outing, having trounced 10 opponents by the astonishing total of 565 points to 6! It had kept Menominee, Marinette, New London, Sheboygan, Ishpeming, Oshkosh, the Milwaukee and Chicago Athletic Clubs, and Stambaugh from scoring, and had yielded a solitary touchdown to Racine in achieving its unblemished record. Although Beloit had outscored its opposition 177 to 68 for a highly creditable showing, it did not figure to be able to match the vaunted Packer power.

Considerable betting support for the Packers came from Beloit neighbor Janesville. It was reported that anywhere from $1,000 to $5,000 was bet on the game and that some of the Bower City people were wagering even money that Green Bay would win by at least 20 points.

There is perhaps only one completely incontestable fact about Sunday's game: that Beloit indeed did score a touchdown on the last play of the first half. As to whether or not the half should have ended *before* that final play is still being vigorously argued, however.

Halfway through the second quarter, Beloit had recovered a Green Bay fumble on the 40-yard line, and Captain Dutch Witte quickly threw the pigskin to Van Kuren to the visitors' 25. Four plunges then earned a first down on the 15, and when fullback Scheibel smashed off tackle to the 5-yard line it was another first down. The crowd jammed along the sidelines erupted with excitement. Three times the AAC team hurled itself against the determined defenses of Green Bay, and each time it was unable to thrust itself into the end zone. And when Scheibel was stopped in his tracks on fourth down, the Packers had seemingly prevented a score. But Beloit Referee Zabell called an off-side penalty against Green Bay, and despite Packer protests the ball was placed down on the 1-yard line.

Still it seemed that the Packers would get through the half without yielding a score when Green Bay timekeeper Wheeler signaled the end of time in the quarter. But even as the Packers were relaxing in relief, Beloit timekeeper McCarthy was maintaining that 5 seconds still remained to be played. The dispute was settled by Zabell in favor of McCarthy. (Both Zabell and umpire Gharrity were from Beloit, head linesman C. N. Murphy from Green Bay.) Accordingly, Beloit had time for one more play—and Walsh quickly snapped the ball back to Scheibel without any signals; Scheibel shot into the line and despite the surging Packers was able to get into the end zone, just as the whistle blew.

Witte (who was given credit by some for scoring the touchdown) then attempted the extra point, but the kick barely got off the ground. Nevertheless, Beloit had 6 points—and they proved to be enough.

So heated were the arguments thereafter, both during the remainder of the game and after it, that the only true picture emerges from the dispatches of journalists representing the 2 contesting communities. Then this furious battle will be fully depicted, for each city viewed the skirmishing in a different light. Indeed, even a neutral observer finds it difficult to properly assess the goings-on.

Hence this account will be interspersed with portions of the accounts written by sportswriters from the Beloit *Daily News* (E. B. Gates) and the Green Bay *Press-Gazette* (whose reporter lists himself only as a "staff correspondent" but who undoubtedly is George Calhoun—both the Packer general manager and a newspaperman). Some additional observations by the relatively unbiased reporter for the Janesville *Gazette* have also been obtained as a further balance to this furiously argued affair.

On one point, all contestants and writers are in agreement— more so, actually, than on the scoring of Beloit's deciding touchdown: that this was a tremendous game of football. As an exulting Gates writes, "it was a game to go down in history," with the AAC winning by "playing a style of football that would make any team in the country proud; Beloit won because of pure fight." He continues lyrically in his *News* story:

> It is doubtful if ever a championship match has been fought in such a setting. Starting shortly before 3 o'clock the final gun wasn't pulled until 5:08 o'clock. As the game wore on, the setting sun sent its rays into the eyes of the defensive players and proved a handicap. Later the mole-skin fighters tore away driving with every plunge nearer to the wonderful sunset sky—a masterpiece of scarlets and purples. Then the deepening dusk, with the steel-springed athletes but blurred figures still fighting up and down the turf. And all at once, as the lines gathered for yet another clash, the spit-flame of the timer's gun cut out against the dark, its sharp crack spoke, and Beloit had won the game.

On the other hand, the *Press-Gazette* account focused more on the officiating than on the beauty of the setting. Readers in Green Bay will have no words minced in the account:

> Capt. [Earl Louis "Curly"] Lambeau's team was robbed of victory by Referee Zabell of Beloit. This official penalized Green Bay three times after touchdowns, refusing to allow the scores. The Packers were twice on the verge of leaving the field but decided to play it out.
>
> Every time the Packers had the ball, the crowd would sweep out on the playing field, leaving practically no room for a forward pass offensive and of course, in this way, putting a big check on the Packers ground gaining machine. Just before the close of the game, McLean got away for a long run, headed goalward, close to the sidelines, when a Beloit spectator gave him a foot and the Packer quarterback fell to the ground. This was just one of the many obstacles that Green Bay had to combat with during their stay in Beloit.

To illustrate his point further, the *Press-Gazette* correspondent secured several comments from Green Bay people immediately after the game. G. A. DeLair was blunt about his feelings: "Nothing short of highway robbery!"

206

Head linesman Murphy, who represented Green Bay on the officiating crew, also made his opinion plain: "I wish to go on record as saying that it was the most deliberate steal I have ever seen. Green Bay had the ball over the goal line for clear touchdowns on three different occasions, and each three times officials ruled off side. It was a cut and dried deal to give Green Bay the worst of it, and they succeeded one hundred per cent."

The Packers' coach, W. J. Ryan, quoted a brief remark by a Janesville businessman, who told him that he had been "over to the robbery this afternoon" in referring to the game.

And one of the Packer players expressed the sentiments of the entire squad when he asserted that "Beloit had the game won before the teams stepped upon the gridiron."

When the teams trotted onto the field, Green Bay won the toss and Lambeau chose to kick off. The Packers immediately stopped Beloit from advancing, forced a punt to McLean at midfield, and then drove to the 5-yard line, where a 15-yard holding penalty by Zabell ended the threat.

Thereafter play seesawed until midway in the second period. The Packers swept upfield on end runs by Lambeau and Gallagher to the Beloit 6. But here 2 plays netted nary a yard, and when McLean passed incomplete into the end zone, Beloit—under the rules—was awarded the ball on the 20.

The AAC promptly punted out of danger to McLean on the 40, but a costly fumble gave the Line City squad possession and led to its game-deciding touchdown as the half ended.

The Packers made their most determined assault in the third quarter. Using wide end runs and a split-buck formation, they penetrated literally to within the shadow of the Beloit goalposts.

At this point, the crowd tightly encircled the field of play, becoming virtually a mob—and so that it was physically impossible to follow the subsequent plays closely. Consequently, the accounts (albeit conflicting!) by the Green Bay and Beloit—and Janesville—newspapers will perhaps better relate the action in this crucial situation. By obtaining those writers' copy, this reporter is able to present their on-the-spot reports of "just what did happen" in the most controversial sequence of plays in the game. Because they, too, had difficulty in following the plays accurately, some discrepancies in their accounts are understandable—especially in consideration of their acknowledged partisanship.

Under the trying crowd conditions, Curly Lambeau 3 times lugged the ball into the end zone, but each time the touchdown was nullified as the referee penalized the Packers back to the 8 for being off side, again for off side to the 13, and once again for motion to the 18. That effectively ended the threat.

But the other 3 accounts give a more vivid description of what transpired.

From the Beloit *Daily News:*

> A desperate Green Bay rally gave Beloit fans heart failure late in the third quarter . . . to within a yard of the Beloit goal. The Beloit line was ruled off side and the distance to the goal divided, giving the Packers first down with only a few inches to go. Three times the Packers were held without gaining an inch. Then Green Bay was penalized when its backfield was ruled in motion and offside. This happened on a play in which a Green Bay back squirmed across the line but the ball had to go back under the penalty. Another smash at the line netted no gain and the Packers decided to try the forward pass. The pass was incomplete behind the goal which counted as a touchdown [sic] for the AACs and gave the Beloit team the ball on its 20-yard line.
>
> Green Bay protested the presence of the crowd on the field and several minutes were consumed while efforts were made to get the fans back of the side lines.

From the Green Bay *Press-Gazette:*

> With the ball resting on Beloit's 5-yard line, Capt. Lambeau bucked tackle for as clean a touchdown as has ever been made on a gridiron. After the whistle blew, Referee Zabell took the ball and set it back two yards claiming the forward motion of the ball had stopped before Green Bay's captain went over the line. It was here the riot started. For a time, it looked as if there would be a great little free-for-all. After a lengthy dispute, the teams went at it once more. Capt. Lambeau warned every man on the Packers to keep his hands to home and guard against off

side. On this play, the Green Bay leader shot across the goal line with three yards to spare. As he did, Zabell once more blew his whistle, called an off side on Green Bay, penalized the Packers 5 yards and gave the ball to Beloit.

This was the straw that broke the camel's back. The Packers came within an inch of leaving the field, but at the last moment decided to fight it out at all costs.

From the Janesville *Gazette:*

Foot by foot, Green Bay pushed onward until they shoved the ball over the line. The joy of the Packers and their rooters was soon dampened, when the referee claimed that a Green Bay man had been off side. With the ball taken back, Green Bay tried some running, but it was forced into a criss-cross sprint and then the referee penalized the visitors again, this time for an out-of-bounds play. A beefing match then followed with the referee and the captain of the Green Bay team chewing the fat over the rule book, and the discovery that the referee is using a 1918 set of rules.

Suffice it to say that Baldy Zabell will not be asked to referee the forthcoming rematch!

Each team had its chances in the final quarter, but neither could score. While the slightly heavier 170-pound-average Packer line was primarily responsible for holding the Gateway City attackers, Green Bay howled that on 2 occasions it was the Beloit crowd that cheated it of touchdowns. Once was when Gallagher made a fine catch of a pass and headed for the goal, only to have the mob bunch ahead of him and stop his progress. Later McLean, as previously chronicled, had broken into the clear but was tripped by a spectator.

Among the more noteworthy performances on the embattled field were those by the 2 quarterbacks, Witte and McLean—the former being particularly outstanding in his high-spiraling punts. Although 4 Green Bay passes were permitted to be completed, the basketball experience of Witte and Phil Phillips also proved extremely helpful in the Maroon defensive backfield. Lambeau and Scheibel were probably the 2 finest rushers of the day, the

Packer captain being extremely versatile, and the latter being a corking good fullback plunger.

Despite their stinging defeat, which spoiled hopes of an undefeated season, it was nevertheless a promising start for the newly organized Packers—and if they could win the rematch next month, it will be balm to their hurts of yesterday (although many feel the rematch will never be played).

Not enough can be said for the part played by Lambeau in making the Packers what they are today, although he is barely 22 years of age. The crinkly-haired Belgian began playing in neighborhood games when the ball was simply a salt sack filled with leaves and dirt. When he went to East High he not only was a great player but unofficially coached the team in his senior year when the regular coach went into the Army. As a freshman at Notre Dame in 1918, he made the varsity under new coach Knute Rockne, was switched from a halfback under George Gipp to fullback, and promptly scored the first touchdown of the opening game against Case. But a bad case of tonsilitis during the winter months made him return home after missing nearly 2 months of school—and when he obtained a job at the Indian Packing Company at $250 a month he forgot college.

August he called an organizational meeting for a football team. Elected captain, he called 3 workouts a week (after supper) starting September 3—some 3 weeks later and just 11 days before the first game.

Through $500 given by Lambeau's boss, Frank Peck, the Indian Packing Company provided blue and gold sweaters and stockings. Little protective equipment has been worn. Indeed, many players feel that such gear interferes with play—and at any rate, few Packers have suffered injuries that kept them from playing.

The players have agreed to divide the profits from the season (they have paid their own doctor bills), and indications are that each of the 21 regulars will receive almost $17 for his efforts during grueling autumn months. Prospects are better for the 1920 season, however. Plans are being made to erect fences and bleachers—and probably to inaugurate a 50-cent admission charge—whereas this year the only means of obtaining money at Hagemeister Brewery park has been to have Manager Calhoun "pass the hat."

XXII

KANSAS CITY CHIEFS VS. OAKLAND RAIDERS
(Game played January 4, 1970)

OAKLAND, CALIF. (Jan. 5, 1970)—A second-place team will represent the American Football League in the Super Bowl next Sunday! That bizarre situation came about when the inspired—and marvelously prepared—Kansas City Chiefs upset favored Oakland yesterday in the finals of the AFL playoffs, 17-7, to earn the right to meet the National Football League's Minnesota Vikings in New Orleans a week hence. It was a most emphatic upset.

Kansas City had finished second in season-long divisional play, but because of the this-year-only playoff format set up by the AFL, it got a crack at the teams that won the Eastern and Western sectors of the league—and it beat them both! A week ago KC dethroned the world champion New York Jets, 13-6, and now it has disposed of an Oakland team that whipped it twice during the regular season, 27-24 and 10-6.

Humbled by the Green Bay Packers, 35-10, in the first Super Bowl game 3 years ago, the Chiefs will no doubt be underdogs again when they meet the Purple Gang of Minnesota next week—but they are a seasoned ball club, attuned to winning the big ones, and surely imbued with determination to avenge that early Super Bowl loss by jolting the NFL representative just as the Jets did a year ago.

For Oakland, it was plain misery. The Raiders (Western division champions for the last 3 years) had won 6 of the 7 games played between the 2 teams up to yesterday, including those twin wins this year. And they cannot help but remember that just a year ago they were ousted from Super Bowl money in another AFL playoff final when the Jets edged them 27-23.

Defense was the key element in Kansas City's win Sunday. The team had an alert secondary and a rarely budged anti-running line. Nothing was more critical, though, than its devastating pass rush. That front-line charge had the dual effect of forcing 4 interceptions (3 in the final quarter) and crippling quarterback Daryle

Lamonica. Lamonica had been thrown for losses only 11 times in the 14 regular-season games, but the Chiefs nailed him 4 times yesterday—3 times by hulking Aaron Brown (a 6-foot-5, 265-pound defensive end who was trouble all day), and once by Curley Culp. Over the campaign, he had thrown 34 TD passes, including last week's playoff rout of Houston (56-7). But early in the second half, Lamonica banged his hand against the helmet of the onrushing Brown and thereafter was never the same. Until then he had been 14 for 27 in a close ball game (7-all), but after a brief respite on the bench, he came back and was a paltry 3 for 18. And Lamonica—a fit Lamonica—is never 3 for 18. He was obviously hurting.

And 3 interceptions in the fourth quarter just as obviously canceled the Oakland attack; the Raiders could not get any kind of a march going. Those interceptions—on the 18, the 10, and the 20—killed any Oakland hopes of victory.

Ironically, Kansas City fumbled the ball away 4 times, but when 4 Raider passes were snapped up it was a standoff in the giveaway department.

The way the game ended was almost symbolic of the way things went for most of the 60 minutes—with Brown driving in on Lamonica on a desperation fourth-down try. The game didn't clock out on the play, but it might as well have. It was as good as ended.

Len Dawson rates kudos for his work in leading the Chiefs to victory and the Super Bowl, although it was by no means a spectacular offensive show. He passed with moderation and hit on his throws. Still, it was his overheads that set things up for KC. His passes led directly to short touchdown smashes by Wendell Hayes (1 yard) and Bob Holmes (5 yards). For the game Dawson was 7 for 17 and 121 yards. Not spectacular, but acceptable.

Actually, the critical play was a 62-yard interception runback by cornerback Emmitt Thomas, which set up Jan Stenerud's 22-yard field goal in the final quarter. Those 3 points iced it, for until then any single long pass connection—or breakaway run—could have tied it for Oakland.

Oakland, even while Lamonica was hale and hearty, was unable to do much on the attack. Its one scoring thrust gave hometown

GAME 19
Chicago Bears vs.
San Francisco 49ers
December 12, 1965

Gayle Sayers (40)
scored his fourth
touchdown of the day
at the start of the
second half when he
took the ball at
midfield and sprinted
50 yards for the 6
points. *(U.P.I.)*

Sayers plunges over
from the 1-yard line for
the fifth of his 6
touchdowns of the day.
(U.P.I.)

As Jim Harvey (70)
blocks Kansas City's
Jim Kearney (46),
Oakland's Charlie
Smith (23) rambles
into the end zone to
score the Raiders' only
touchdown of the day.
(U.P.I.)

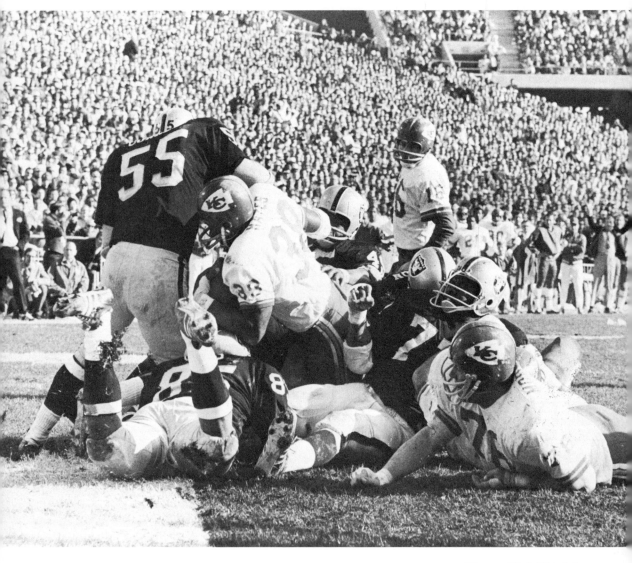

Kansas City's Wendel
Hayes (38) crashes
across the goal line for
a second-period
touchdown. Jan
Stenerud's point after
tied the score. *(U.P.I.)*

GAME 23
New York Giants vs.
Chicago Bears
December 6, 1925

Chicago's Joe
Sternaman scored a
first-period touchdown
and kicked the extra
point himself. *(U.P.I.)*

Sternaman gallops 18
yards for his second
touchdown of the
afternoon in the third
period. *(U.P.I.)*

McBride (36) of the
Giants evades Chicago
tacklers for a short gain
in the third period.
(U.P.I.)

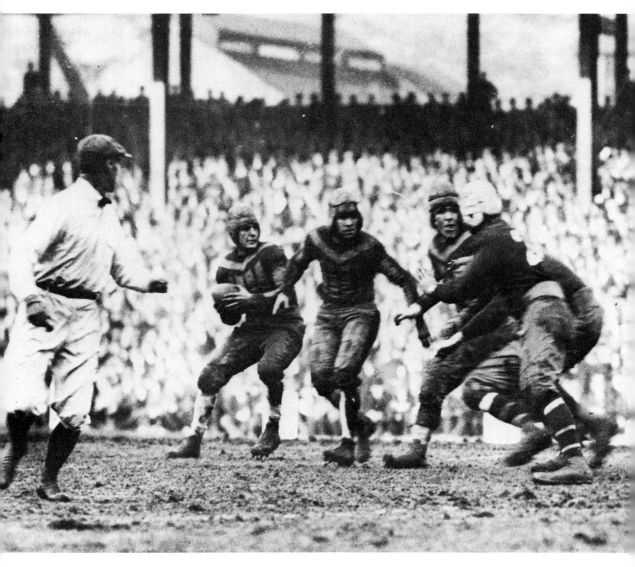

Red Grange is about to
toss a 14-yard pass to
Walquist to set up
Chicago's second
touchdown. *(U.P.I.)*

fans early gaiety in the first quarter, Charlie Smith darting home from the 4 for an opening TD that made it a 7-0 ball game. (George Blanda kicked the PAT.) But from then on, the Raiders just could not do anything against that formidable Kansas City defense. Only sporadically could they even remotely threaten.

Actually, Oakland had marvelous chances. It received 3 fumbles (2 by Holmes, 1 by Dawson handing off to Hayes) late in the game that offered great opportunities. But that KC pass rush harassed Lamonica, his throwing hand was bothering him besides, and it all added up to zero on the scoreboard.

Down by 7-0 after the first quarter, KC finally moved in the second quarter. Dawson incredibly missed on 7 straight passes in the first half, but he came up with a crucial toss to wide receiver Frank Pitts for a 41-yard strike down to the 1-yard line—and from there Hayes slammed home. Stenerud then kicked the PAT and it was 7-all, and so it remained through the remainder of the half.

Hayes, incidentally, led KC runners with a niggardly 35 yards, an indication of the feebleness of the ground efforts by both teams. KC netted 86 yards and Oakland a meager 79.

Oakland got 2 scoring chances early in the second half but neither time could put points on the board. The rugged Kansas City defensive unit kept the Raiders from penetrating beyond the 30 on both occasions and forced them to go for field-goal tries from the 39 and the 40. George Blanda, the amazing 42-year-old NFL "castoff" from the Chicago Bears who has done so remarkably both as a Raider reserve quarterback and a place-kicker, tried both kicks but neither was good.

Blanda replaced the injured Lamonica at the QB slot shortly before his second attempt. The injury came on a crashing charge by the huge Brown on a play that Lamonica felt could have been a big one. "I had Larry Todd one-on-one on a linebacker and it could have been all the way, but I banged Brown's helmet when I followed through and jammed my thumb, and both knuckles of two of my fingers swelled up," he lamented later in the locker room. "I threw some good balls after I got hurt, but to follow through you have to put some zing on the ball, and I just couldn't do it all the time." Lamonica pointed out that one of his passes "hung" and was picked off, and he simply could not throw the ball with his accustomed style. He considered rolling out, but felt that "if you have to revert to that, you pretty much defeat your own purpose as a passer."

Later in the third quarter, after his second field-goal miss, Blanda missed on a great scoring chance for the third time. The ball was on the Kansas City 24 and it was second and 10. Blanda went back to pass and tried to throw to Warren Wells in the end zone—but to his consternation saw Thomas snatch the ball for an interception. However, instead of downing the ball to give Kansas City possession on the 20, Thomas daringly tried to run it out of the end zone but could get only as far as the 6-yard line.

KC was in trouble when Holmes was dropped for a 4-yard loss back to the 2 on second down. But Lennie Dawson came up with an audacious play in this critical third-and-14 situation on the 2-yard line—a play that just about everybody later acknowledged was probably the game-breaker. The veteran quarterback had to drop far back into his end zone to get the ball away on a pass primarily meant for Holmes. But Holmes, cutting across the Oakland secondary from the left, collided with someone around the middle and was unable to get free for the catch. Luckily, Dawson—who had to get rid of the ball quickly—saw Otis Taylor near the sideline and instantly decided to throw to him, so that even if the pass missed it would sail harmlessly out of bounds. Taylor had been lined up in a slot between guard and tackle, which confused the Raiders just long enough to free him. He got away from classy cornerback Willie Brown with just enough leeway to outleap him for the ball on a hurtling catch that catapulted him out of bounds into teammates standing in front of the KC bench. "I realized I was pretty close to the sidelines, but I didn't know how close," Taylor said later. He made, as Dawson put it, "a great catch." That moved the ball from a potential disaster area on the 2 out to the 37.

And the Chiefs immediately capitalized on the situation. First Dawson again went to Holmes in the air. This time the husky running back got clear for a big 23-yard gain into Oakland territory. Then Dawson went to Taylor on a deep strike, and when Nemiah Wilson was called for interference it gave KC first down on the 7-yard line. "I never pushed him," Wilson remonstrated later, but Taylor disagreed—and so, of course, did the officials.

From there the Chiefs stayed on the ground. On the first 2 plays, the determined Raiders held Holmes to a paltry 2 yards—but on the third try the 220-pound slammer scooted wide to the left and swept in for the score. When Stenerud booted the placement it was 14-7. At the time it hardly seemed a safe margin, but those points proved to be sufficient.

Stenerud later kicked a 22-yard field goal in the fourth quarter that was the clincher. As noted earlier, it was a 62-yard gallop with an intercepted pass by Thomas that put the Chiefs in position for that kick, for the offense generally was unable to generate anything consistent in the way of a march. Fumbles kept messing things up whenever the Chiefs seemed about to move the ball for any distance—or, for that matter, even as they initiated an assault.

But while fumbles thwarted the Kansas City attack, interceptions stymied the Oakland offense to the dismay of the record Coliseum throng of 54,544. Lamonica had one picked off by Kearney at the 18-yard line, another by Marsalis at the 10, and a third by Thomas at the 20. And this despite the absence of free safety Johnny Robinson in the Chiefs' lineup after he hurt his ribs hurtling into a cameraman. Willie Mitchell, however, did a first-rate job filling in for him.

That awesome KC pass rush, of course, had much to do with those interceptions, and Lamonica lauded it as being the best the Chiefs had ever shown. Defensive ends Brown and Jerry Mays both were tremendous. Said Mays of Brown: "I think he had a fantastic game—the greatest pass rush I've ever seen. I know every time I was rushing, I saw Aaron coming like gangbusters. Aaron and I took more of an inside rush today than ever before. We figured if he wanted to roll out, we'd gamble and let him—but we knew inside pressure would bother him more." Stram approved their tactics, believing that when Lamonica is pressured "he isn't as good."

So the Chiefs, for all their runner-up status, are Super Bowlers. They had been a modest 11-3 in regular-season play, behind Oakland's superior 12-1-1 slate in the Western division. Now, after

2 playoff wins, they will take a 13-3 record against Minnesota's 14-2 mark.

Despite being members of the younger American Football League, the Chiefs nevertheless are actually "older" than next Sunday's foe! Kansas City's franchise dates back to 1960, Minnesota's to 1961. KC owner Lamar Hunt organized the AFL that year, an even decade ago. And when the 1970 fall campaign begins, the American Football League will be no more, having been absorbed by merger with the NFL. So Kansas City will have an opportunity of evening the score in Super Bowl play between the two leagues, two wins apiece.

The Scoring:

Kansas City	0	7	7	3	—	17
Oakland	7	0	0	0	—	7

Oak.—Smith 4, run (Blanda kick)
KC—Hayes 1, run (Stenerud kick)
KC—Holmes 5, run (Stenerud kick)
KC—FG Stenerud 22

The Statistics:

	KC	Oak.
First downs	13	12
Rushing yardage	86	79
Passing yardage	121	154
Passes	7-17	17-45
Own passes intercepted	0	4
Punting	8-43	6-49
Fumbles lost	4	0
Penalties	43	45

XXIII

NEW YORK GIANTS VS. CHICAGO BEARS
(Game played December 6, 1925)

NEW YORK, N.Y. (Dec. 6, 1925)—Out of a little Midwestern town came a fiery-haired youth who took the big city by storm. The largest crowd that ever witnessed a professional football game swarmed into the Polo Grounds yesterday to see the far-famed Red Grange in action. It was the first appearance of the Galloping Ghost in this city, and 70,000 people streamed into the stadium that lies below Coogan's Bluff and saw the Red Rover lead the Chicago Bears to a 19-7 victory over their own New York Giants.

High honors have been heaped on the bright brow of the college football star who turned financier, but nothing could have attested to his popularity as did the outpouring of New York citizenry. Seldom, if ever, before has the Polo Grounds, where practically every sport but polo has been staged, accommodated such a crowd. There were just so many tickets, and they were all bought. But that didn't stop the overflow that wedged into vacant corners, flooded in 2 and 3 deep along the rear railings, and spilled over onto the sidelines. The game was covered by more than 100 reporters from all parts of the country, from as far west as St. Louis, Missouri.

Had the New York Giants played the Chicago Bears without Red Grange among those on the field, it would have been just another football game. But the redhead in action was a spectacle that attracted spectators from almost every walk of life.

And "The Iceman" delivered, despite the slippery footing of the water-soaked field. He deliberately plunged through the line, he hurled passes into waiting arms for further advances, he snatched the ball out of the air while Giants swarmed around him, and finally, to cap the climax, he intercepted a forward pass in the final period and streaked down the sideline for 30 yards and a touchdown.

There was more than glory and victory in his accomplishments, however, for some $30,000 was added to his rapidly growing bankroll. Altogether Grange advanced the ball, either directly or indirectly, 128 yards. At the rate of the reported payment, the turf of the Polo Grounds was worth approximately $230 a yard, which made it even more valuable than Florida real estate.

There was never any doubt about what brought forth the great gathering. While Grange was in the game, the spectators strained forward eagerly, watching every move he made, waiting for him to break loose from the alert and ever watchful Giants for one of his famous twisting, squirming runs. They yelled for the Giants to get away and they yelled for the Giants to stop him. Every time the ball was snapped into the Chicago backfield, the throng half rose with the shout of "There he goes!" If a big white "77" showed on the back of the runner, they stood up and kept on yelling; if any other number showed they settled back again.

When Grange left the contest in the middle of the second period, the thousands watched with only half interest. When he failed to appear at any time in the third period, a kind of lassitude swept over the stands. And when the final period started with the main attraction still on the sidelines, an inevitable chant went up from the bleacherites, gathered force as it was taken up by those in the reserved seats, and echoed across the field: "We want Grange! We want Grange!"

Then Grange came back. Once more the excitement and the thrill that the crowd came for was in the atmosphere, and once more the spectators leaned forward in eager anticipation. Their hopes and dreams were fulfilled shortly after the last quarter began.

The Giants, trailing by 6 points, were struggling desperately, almost frantically, to keep intact their winning streak that had reached 7 straight victories. A moment before, they had found themselves in the shadow of their own goalposts, forced there by Grange's plunges and passes. They had managed to shake off those dread symbols of danger that rose white and glaring behind them by a frantic forward pass. But they passed once too often. The next time they hurled the ball, the tall, lean, knock-kneed figure of Red Rover flashed across the turf, splashed through a puddle, and leaped high in the air. His long arms clutched the ball and he was off in the opposite direction, swinging smoothly where the

226

going was rough, breaking into the open and sweeping on 35 yards to another touchdown for the Bears.

That one dash over the muddy field was enough to satisfy the throng. That one scamper gave them what they came to see. That one sight of the modern Mercury of the gridiron made old men, young boys, and bright-eyed ladies turn to each other and pronounce Grange all that he had been advertised to be. It also cut off the last chance of a New York victory, but nobody seemed to care about that. They had come to see the phantom in action, and they were satisfied.

Grange is not to be blamed for remaining on the sidelines during the third period and part of the second. He has played 6 football games in the past 15 days, and he still has contests scheduled for Washington, Boston, Pittsburgh, Detroit, and Chicago before next Saturday night. The way to a fortune in football may not be long, but it is extremely exhausting—even for an iceman. It is estimated that in his 5 games as a member of the salaried brigade, Grange has accumulated something over $82,000.

The thousands began assembling in the home of the Giants the minute the gates for bleacher tickets were thrown open. The first rush came from a swarm of small boys who had waited long to gain admission and a point of vantage for the game. Red Grange to most of them meant more than President Coolidge. Perhaps Babe Ruth was better known, but even that is questionable.

The bleachers were filled in a flash, and then the steady stream of reserve-seat ticket holders started pouring in. Gradually the great stands filled. An hour before game time, long lines led to every entrance gate, and even an hour after the game started there still was a steady stream of spectators finding their way to their seats.

The field and stands were decorated for the occasion. Gay bunting floated from the field boxes, gold and blue in honor of the visiting Chicago Bears, red and blue in respect for the home-town Giants—purple, yellow, and scarlet just to add color to the scene. Even the goalposts were decorated with the rival colors, and an innovation was introduced when boys changed the pennants on the uprights whenever the teams changed goals.

Overhead it was bright and balmy. No more perfect football day has dawned this season so far as the weather was concerned. Only the rain-soaked, mud-caked field prevented perfection. The storms, rains, and drizzles of the past few days left the gridiron wet and slippery and a handicap to Grange, who is at his best on a dry field and in the open. He had to confine most of his activities to line plunges and throwing and receiving passes. Even then he had to travel with extra weight, as his muddy feet looked as if they were wrapped in big, brown bandages after he had been on the field a few minutes.

Only a cheering section was needed to give the spectacle all the trimmings of a big college game. Oh yes, and they left the goalposts standing at the end of the contest. There was a band, there were the massed thousands, and there were the ever-present speculators demanding 2 and 3 times the face value for choice seats. As usual, they got their price.

The appearance of the Bears in golden jerseys caused the first excitement, and every pair of eyes searched the field for the famous "77," which belongs as much to Red Grange as "57" does to Mr. Heinz. He was easy to find. All one had to do was follow the course of the photographers. And once the game started, the great Grange was never out of sight until he retired from the field of action.

The first time the Bears got possession, they started a 62-yard march for their first touchdown. Most of these yards were credited to Walquist and Joe Sternaman, who took the ball over the goal for the score. Grange contributed only 9 yards on 2 plunges.

The redhead played a more prominent part in the second touchdown. Starting from his own 40-yard line, he ploughed through the red and blue line for gains of 6, 3, and 2 yards; he leaped in the air while 3 New York players swarmed around him and caught a pass for a gain of 23 yards; he threw a 14-yard pass to Walquist and then led the way for Sternaman to make the score on an end run. It was Sternaman who carried the ball across, but Grange ran the inteference, and a last lunge at the last man who barred the way cleared the path for his teammate.

Before he retired from the game, Grange did a few other things worth mentioning. A long pass by the Giants was on its way to a resting place in the arms of a receiver when Grange darted in and knocked it down. He caught a punt and stepped out of a tangled mass to gain 9 yards, leaving a heap of disappointed Giants in his wake, and he split the New York line open and swung through for 15 yards before he was stopped in his longest run from scrimmage during the day.

After that he retired until the fourth quarter; during his absence the Bears could make no further progress while the Giants threatened constantly to take the lead with another touchdown, their first having been made in the second period on a sustained drive of 69 yards, most of which was covered by 2 passes from McBride to Romar.

But when Grange came back, the Bears took up the attack once more; starting from their own 30-yard line, they marched down the field to within 1 yard of the New York goal. There Grange was stopped on a plunge, but he made up for it a moment later when he intercepted a forward pass and wove his way down the sideline while the crowd cheered him to the echo.

The Scoring:

Chicago Bears	12	0	0	7	—	19
New York Giants	0	7	0	0	—	7

Touchdowns: (Bears) J. Sternaman (2), Grange.
               (Giants) White.

Points After Touchdown: (Bears) J. Sternaman (drop kick).
                            (Giants) McBride (placement).